ELVIS
THE LEGEND AND THE MUSIC

ELVIS
THE LEGEND AND THE MUSIC

JOHN TOBLER
RICHARD WOOTTON

Crescent Books
New York

Photographic acknowledgments
All the photographs in this book have been supplied by the
Official Elvis Presley Fan Club of Great Britain except those on
the following pages: Cyrus Andrews, London 104 bottom;
Colour Library International, London 131; De Wynters Ltd,
London 171, 172 left; Frank Driggs Collection, New York 128
top, 129 top; Flair Photography, Bushey Heath 52; Hamlyn
Group Picture Library, London 21; Kobal Collection, London
16; National Film Archive 53, 132; Popperfoto, London 144;
Rex Features, London, front cover, 29; Syndication International, London 36, 41 left, 45, 46 top, 46 bottom, 55 top, 100
top, 152, 169, 170.

First English edition published by
Deans International Publishing
52–54 Southwark Street, London SE1 1UA
A division of The Hamlyn Publishing Group Limited
London · New York · Sydney · Toronto

This edition is published by Crescent Books
Distributed by Crown Publishers, Inc.
h g f e d c b a

Printed in Italy

Library of Congress Cataloging in Publication Data

Tobler, John., Wooton, Richard
  Elvis: the legend and the music.
  1. Presley, Elvis, 1935–1977. 2. Singers—
United States—Biography. I. Title.
ML420.P96T65 1982   784.5'4'00924   [B]   82-12703
ISBN 0-517-39150-3

CONTENTS

FROM TUPELO TO MEMPHIS

Elvis Presley, the man who was to become the first and biggest superstar of the rock'n'roll era, was born in very humble circumstances in East Tupelo, Mississippi, on January 8, 1935. His parents, Vernon and Gladys Presley, lived in a sparsely furnished two-room wooden cabin and were so close to the breadline that they were unable to pay the doctor who presided at their son's birth.

Nineteen years later, the same Elvis Presley made his first commercial recordings for the Sun record label in Memphis, launching a career that would result in his becoming one of the most photographed and reviewed figures in entertainment history. As a result, a great deal is known about his public life. His private life, too, at least from the time he came to fame in

1954 until his sadly premature death in 1977, is also well documented. Surprisingly, however, little first-hand information about Elvis's background and upbringing is available.

Writers refrained from making any serious investigations into Presley's early days until several years after the release of his first records. A major reason for this was that it was presumed that few people in the 1950s were interested in investigative articles about such apparently fleeting subjects as rock'n'rollers. Additionally, the genre was brand new, and therefore no tradition of serious rock journalism existed. This meant that interviews rarely delved deeper than questions about favourite foods, colours and music, with the occasional adventurous

The plaque outside Elvis Presley's birthplace in Tupelo, Mississippi.

The first known photograph of Elvis, aged two.

enquiry into physical preferences as regards special friends of the opposite sex.

By the time the demand for more detailed information had grown, Elvis had virtually ceased to grant interviews. The select group who might have been able to provide further enlightenment were either dead, or refused to discuss the matter, or had forgotten the relevant details with the passing of time.

In the wake of Elvis's death there arose a sudden willingness and enthusiasm on the part of those who knew him to 'spill the beans' – although in many cases failing memories and personal motives sometimes led to a drastic reinterpretation of what were generally believed to be 'the facts'. Nevertheless, the more determined researchers uncovered some interesting written documentation about Presley's childhood and adolescence, which has been set alongside a digest of the verbal evidence sifted from Elvis's family, friends and contemporaries.

While it will never be possible to provide a comprehensive and totally accurate account of the first nineteen years of his life, enough information is now available to paint a general picture of his childhood and adolescence. This will in turn give some indication as to why he achieved such huge success, and will also help to shed light on the progress and development of both his career and his private life.

Our story begins in the north-east portion of the state of Mississippi, an area whose original inhabitants were Chickasaw Indians (the name 'Tupelo' is derived from the Chickasaw word for 'lodging place', which is 'topala'). In the early part of the nineteenth century a few white settlers, of mainly British descent, discovered the area and signed a treaty with the indigenous Indians. By 1832 they had forced the Indians to leave, at which point a rush of new settlers migrated there.

Most of the new arrivals earned a living from the land, cultivating both food crops such as peas and corn, and materials such as cotton, and even a century later primitive farming remained a main source of employment for a major portion of the population of north-east Mississippi. The great majority were sharecroppers, working land that belonged to others with

whom they shared the profits – the work was long and arduous and the rewards often seemed pitifully small. America was midway through the Great Depression of the Thirties, and those unfortunate enough to live in rural areas were particularly deprived as a result both of the paucity of money and of the lack of work of the type that might lead to an improvement in the quality of life.

Vernon Elvis Presley and Gladys Love Smith were both from share-cropping families whose ancestors had originally settled in the Carolinas but had subsequently moved west. (The Presley family has been traced back by a genealogical research organization to an English or Irish immigrant named David Pressley who landed in North Carolina around 1740; the spelling of the family name altered somewhere along the line, although the pronunciation of the original was retained.)

Vernon's parents, Jessie McClowell Presley and Minnie Mae Hood, had lived in Fulton, Mississippi. Vernon had been born there in 1916, but the family moved to East Tupelo following the First World War, when the farm on which Vernon's parents worked was sold. The Smith family, meanwhile, had lived in Saltillo – where Gladys was born in 1912 – but had moved south to East Tupelo at the start of the Depression in search of some other kind of work than agriculture. Gladys found employment as a sewing machinist, initially making shirts at the Tupelo Garment Factory but later moving up to Reed's Department Store. Her working hours were long and even in a good week her earnings might amount to as little as $13 – hardly riches, but certainly considerably more than the wage she could have expected to earn working on a farm.

The rural areas in the 1930s were poor but Tupelo was an affluent town where thriving shops and businesses could be found. The quite separate East Tupelo, on the other hand, provided dwellings for those at the lower end of the social scale. No one with sufficient resources to avoid the area would have chosen to live there. A major natural shortcoming of the area was its proximity to several creeks prone to frequently overflowing their inadequate banks, as a result of which, most of the local buildings were elevated on bricks or

wooden stilts in order to prevent an unwelcome tide of flotsam being deposited in the houses every few months.

Vernon lived in a two-room house on Old Saltillo Road (although the term 'road' apparently erred on the generous side) with his parents, his brother Vester, and his three sisters. Gladys lived in a slightly larger house on nearby Berry Street with her parents, her five sisters and her two brothers, Gladys herself being the second youngest of the brood. After she and Vernon met their courtship was fairly brief, and little time seems to have been wasted between the decision to marry and the actual plighting of the troth. By all accounts, the dark-haired girl and her blond lover made a handsome couple, and on June 17, 1933, they made the journey to Pontotoc, some twenty miles west of Tupelo, to be married. Their obvious distress that Gladys, who was twenty-one, was four years older than Vernon led to their giving false ages, which were entered on the marriage licence, Vernon claiming to be twenty-two and Gladys nineteen.

Married life for the Presleys began with them sharing the small Saltillo Road house with Vernon's parents, but when Gladys discovered a year later that she was pregnant the couple made plans for a

house of their own. Vernon was working at that time for a dairy farmer named Orville S. Bean, driving a truck and delivering milk to local East Tupelo homes, and Bean provided the money for a house for the Presleys, which Vernon built with help from his father and brother, the initial finance being repaid to Bean in the form of rent.

The house was constructed in a similar style to many others in East Tupelo – thirty feet long and containing two square rooms, a bedroom at the front and a kitchen at the rear, along with a small porch. The walls were wooden, but a brick chimney stack was provided to service a fire in the front room and a stove at the back. The property lacked a bathroom, the toilet was outside, and the only running water available had to be obtained from a communal tap shared with neighbours.

The couple had hardly been opulent when they first married, but after they moved into their own house financial matters deteriorated even further. Gladys was forced to abandon her job, leaving Vernon's salary as their sole source of income at a time when one or possibly two extra mouths would soon require to be fed – Gladys was convinced that she was to become the mother of twins, both of

An historic birth certificate.

which would be boys, and chose matching names some time before their scheduled arrival. These were Jessie Garon and Elvis Aaron (Elvis being Vernon's middle name and Jessie that of his father).

There was no question of hospitalization for Gladys, as she and Vernon were simply unable to afford it. A local doctor, Dr. William Robert Hunt, attended the birth at the Presley house. Hunt always made notes concerning births he supervised; however, details relevant to the Presley twins who were born on January 8, 1935, were only revealed recently (in 1980) when Dr. Hunt's daughter discovered the jottings made by her father. These divulge that at 4.00 a.m. Gladys produced a stillborn boy and that thirty-five minutes later she gave birth to a second boy who survived. Dr. Hunt also observed that the name of the living baby was Elvis Aaron – in fact the generally accepted spelling of Elvis's second name, although his birth certificate registered it as 'Aron'. (This was almost certainly a spelling mistake and in later years Elvis

himself always spelt his name with two 'a's.) He further observed that the family could not afford to pay his fifteen-dollar fee.

Not unnaturally, Gladys was extremely distraught that only one of her sons was alive, and her distress was further enhanced by the subsequent discovery that she would be unable to bear any more offspring. The body of Jessie Garon was placed in a cardboard box, and kept overnight in the front room of the Presley house, before being buried the following day in an unmarked grave, next to a tree, in Priceville Cemetery, north-east of Tupelo.

One result of this unfortunate chapter of events was that Gladys became extremely protective of her surviving son, much of whose early life was spent in close proximity to his mother, and a very strong emotional attachment grew up between the two. 'My mama never let me out of her sight', recalled Elvis many years later, 'and I couldn't go down to the creek with the other kids. Sometimes, when I was

10

Two-year-old Elvis with his parents, Gladys and Vernon.

little, I used to run off, and then mama would whip me, and that made me think she didn't love me.' Gladys appears to have had a terrible fear that something involving fire or water would harm Elvis (the anxiety about fire was justifiable since many East Tupelo homes were highly susceptible to accidental conflagration due to their wooden construction), and this paranoia was passed on to her son. Friends of the family recall two particular incidents when the infant Elvis became terrified for the safety of his father, the first being when Vernon dived into a lake and the second when he rushed into a neighbour's burning home in an attempt to salvage some furniture. 'Elvis was so sure that his daddy was going to get hurt that he screamed and cried', Gladys told a reporter during the 1950s. 'I had to hold him to keep him from running in after Vernon. So I said sharp, "Elvis, you just stop that. He's all right. Your daddy knows what he's doing." He quieted right down.'

Although ultra-protective of her son, Gladys gave him as much as she could afford. However, she was strict with his upbringing, insisting that he be polite to his elders. He would always stand up when adults entered the room, and would address them as 'sir' or 'ma'am', traits that had become second nature by the time he became a rock star in the 1950s when his answers to the questions posed by interviewers or disc jockeys were always prefaced by the appropriate polite epithet.

Despite their severe shortage of money, Vernon and Gladys scrimped and saved to provide the best they could for their only son. Vernon worked long hours, but his pay was always low, and there were few opportunities to earn extra cash. This is perhaps some minor justification for his involvement in a foolish minor crime for which he was apprehended in 1937: along with Gladys's brother Travis Smith and another accomplice named Lether Gable, Vernon was charged with forgery after altering the figures on a cheque given to him by his benefactor, Orville Bean. Reports vary about precise details and the

Pre-teen Elvis outside his birthplace in Tupelo.

they were subjected to harsh punishment if they slackened their pace. The prison achieved notoriety some years later when Mose Allison wrote and recorded a song about it *Parchman Farm*. (Both his song and an adaptation by the Kingston Trio, titled *Parchman Farm Blues*, become popular.)

It has never been revealed precisely how long Vernon was imprisoned – not surprisingly, he was less than effusive about his indiscretion after Elvis came to fame – although we can be virtually certain that he served a good deal less than the full three years. He probably earned remission for good behaviour, which may have resulted in him actually being discharged from prison after serving less than one year. Meanwhile, Orville Bean had turned Gladys and the three-year-old Elvis out of the family home as soon as Vernon changed his plea to 'guilty', so they moved in next door with Vernon's parents Jessie and Minnie Mae while Gladys returned to work as a seamstress.

Elvis accompanied his mother almost everywhere, the local church being no exception. The First Assembly Of God Church – an unimpressive one-storey wood cabin only marginally larger than the houses surrounding it – could be found at 206 Adams Street, a short distance from Old Saltillo Road. The church had Pentecostal leanings and the congregation were not only permitted, but positively encouraged, to contribute to the worship, sometimes rocking back and forth in their pews and exclaiming 'Praise the Lord' or 'Thanks be to God' in support of their lively and impassioned preachers. Gospel music was an important influence on Elvis's vocal style, for some of his earliest and most vivid memories related to the church and particularly to the music he heard there:

'Since I was two years old all I knew was gospel music, and that music became such a part of my life that it was as natural as dancing. A way to escape from problems, and my way of release . . . In church, I loved to hear the choir – my mother told me that when I was two years old I would slide off her lap and stand there singing. I could carry a tune, even though I didn't know the words – maybe I wasn't always in tune, but you could sure hear me above the rest! When I was four

sum involved, though all agree that it was relatively small, particularly as far as the opulent Bean was concerned (one account suggests that Vernon sold Bean a calf for four dollars and later changed the amount of the cheque to forty dollars). Vernon's relatives endeavoured to convince Bean to drop the charges, but being the kind of man he was, he persisted with the case, determined that the trio be punished.

When Presley, Smith and Gable appeared in court in May 1938, they changed their original 'not guilty' plea to one of 'guilty', possibly expecting a more lenient sentence as a result. If this was their motive it was ill-conceived, for they were each sentenced to three years in the state prison of Mississippi, the infamous Parchman Penitentiary. This was a labour camp where prisoners (most of whom were poverty-stricken blacks) were forced to spend long hours working in the cotton fields. Their treatment was inhuman, and

or five, all I looked forward to was Sundays when we'd all go to church. I loved the old church, filled with sunlight, and the security of my mother and father beside me. That was the only singing training I had – I never took lessons.'

The Presley family also attended 'camp meetings' and 'religious revivals', where the demeanour of both worshippers and preachers was considerably more animated than in the more solemn confines of church, and the behaviour of some of the preachers Elvis saw in action appears to have played a significant role in his stage movements, which were deemed so controversial in the 1950s. As Elvis later remembered, 'We used to go to those religious sing-ins all the time, and the preachers used to cut up all over the place. And that was how I was introduced to the onstage wiggle – the preachers did it! And the congregation loved it. Why, I even remember one day a preacher jumped on the piano – I never did that!'

In his early years, Elvis heard little other than gospel songs, but when a radio arrived in the Presley household he discovered new songs, initially the country music to which his parents listened, but as time passed inquisitive spinning of the dial also brought black R&B (rhythm & blues) to his ears.

Elvis began attending school locally at the age of five, his ever-protective mother seeing him to and from the school premises every day across Highway 78. He appears to have been an almost totally unremarkable pupil, who excelled at nothing in particular and did little to attract attention to himself, to the point that when he had become famous few of his teachers could recall anything about their erstwhile charge.

However, one event did stand out, and that involved Elvis's first public performance. His teacher at the time, a Mrs. J. C. Grimes, asked her class whether anyone knew prayers or hymns, whereupon the normally shy Elvis volunteered to perform some songs he knew. One of them, *Old Shep*, certainly wasn't a hymn but rather a country music hit (which he had obviously heard on the radio). Impressed by his performance of the tear-jerking song about a boy and his beloved dog, Mrs. Grimes took Elvis to see the Principal of the school, Mr. J. D. Cole.

Elvis at the age of 12 or 13.

Equally affected, Mr. Cole arranged to take the boy to the Mississippi/Alabama Fair and Dairy Show. One of the activities at the Show was a talent contest which was broadcast over the local radio station, WELO – in addition to the Fair providing the setting for the first public performance by Elvis Presley, it also became the scene of his broadcasting debut. The show apparently took place on October 3, 1945, when Elvis was ten and a half years old, and due to his inability to reach the microphone, he was obliged to stand on a chair to sing *Old Shep* unaccompanied. The performance won him second prize – five dollars and free rides at the Fair.

This was the sole reported occasion of Elvis singing in public during his pre-teen years: however, it is clear that he was becoming increasingly interested in music, for large portions of his spare time were spent listening to the radio – which was probably just as well, as Mr. and Mrs.

Elvis, at the age of 13, poses in his cowboy suit.

Presley were still very poor and if anything, worse off than when their son had been born.

Vernon struggled with a succession of badly paid jobs and the family moved house frequently, on occasion having nowhere to live and thus being obliged to descend on relatives. A move to Tupelo proper in 1946 failed to improve matters, and the family habitually lived on the poor side of town. Nevertheless, Elvis remained the most important feature of the lives of his doting parents, who continued to do their best to provide their son with everything he wanted.

Obviously, this was not always possible, and one particular item that Elvis desired and his parents could not afford would later have far-reaching consequences – for one of his birthdays, the youth asked for a bicycle. Elvis later recalled 'I really wanted that bicycle, but daddy couldn't afford one, so he bought me a guitar which cost about twelve bucks. I know even that was a great sacrifice, and he went without smokes for several weeks'. Learning to play his new acquisition was the next step, and two of Elvis's uncles, Uncle Johnny (his mother's brother) and Uncle Vester (his father's brother, who had incidentally married Gladys's sister Cletis), knew the rudiments of guitar-playing and taught their nephew a few chords. Elvis, however, claimed: 'I learned most of it from the radio station in Tupelo, and from other people's phonograph records. I used to listen to the radio quite a lot, and I loved records by Sister Rosetta Tharpe and country singers like Roy Acuff, Ernest Tubb, Ted Daffan, Jimmie Rodgers, Jimmy Davis and Bob Wills.'

One of the Tupelo radio stations, WELO, was located very near one of the Presley homes, in Mobile Alley, and the town's only notable musician, Carvel Lee Ausborn (professionally known as Mississippi Slim) broadcast live from the station every Saturday. Elvis undoubtedly heard his performances and may well have known him quite well, as Carvel's younger brother James was a pupil in the same class as Elvis at school. To estimate Mississippi Slim's musical influence, if any, on Elvis could only be a matter for conjecture, and any musical relationship shared by the two would inevitably have been short-lived as the Presleys soon moved away from the area.

In 1948 Vernon was unemployed, and since there seemed little prospect of any worthwhile job falling vacant in Tupelo, he and Gladys decided to leave their home, their friends and their relatives to try for a fresh start in Memphis, a big city about 100 miles away in the neighbouring state of Tennessee. Vernon had actually worked for a short time in Memphis during the Second World War, at a defence plant, and the mood of the family was as optimistic as circumstances allowed, as Elvis noted when remembering

their departure: 'We were broke, man, broke, and we left Tupelo overnight. Dad packed all our belongings in boxes and put them on the top and in the trunk of our 1939 Plymouth.

'Things just had to get better.' They didn't, and for a while matters were even worse.

The Presley's first home in Memphis was a single room in a large house at 572 Poplar Avenue, probably the most depressing place of all the many inhabited by them. Poplar Avenue lay about a mile from the Mississippi river and close to the centre of Memphis. It had once been an area where wealthy Memphians had lived, and all the houses were consequently large, but as the buildings began to deteriorate with age, the well-to-do had moved elsewhere. 572 Poplar Avenue was typical of the area's decline, having become a slum property divided into sixteen units. Apart from having to share a bathroom with several other families, the Presleys' room was infested with a variety of bugs, and everything it contained was in need of serious repair (especially the electrical wiring, which was potentially lethal). Elvis was enrolled at the nearest school, Humes High, a three-storey building accommodating 1600 pupils. The school so terrified him at first that he ran home as soon as Vernon had left him outside the principal's office, but he gradually became more accustomed to it. Nevertheless, very little is known about his time there before his final two years,

Elvis, at the age of 15, in the Army Cadet Corps at Humes High School.

One of Elvis's favourite film stars was Tony Curtis, pictured here in 1947 when he was 22.

which saw him beginning to behave in a manner that made him very noticeable.

Elvis's mother continued to behave very protectively towards her son, and Elvis once said that she continued to accompany him to school until he was fifteen years old. Even such an indignity failed to affect their relationship, which remained extremely intense: Elvis knew that if he ever had anything on his mind his mother would be available to discuss it, whatever the time. 'I could wake her any hour of the night, and if I was worried or troubled about something, she'd get up and try to help me. I used to get angry at her when I was growing up – it's a natural thing, isn't it? A young person wants to go somewhere, do something, and your mother won't let you so you think "Well, what's wrong with you?" but later on in years you find out that she was right, that she was only doing it to protect you from getting into trouble and getting hurt, and I'm very happy that she was kinda strict.'

Vernon got a job as a packer at the United Paint Factory on Concord Avenue, where he earned around $40 per week: still not much, but certainly an improvement on what he'd made in Tupelo. Things gradually began to improve for the Presleys. They must have been overjoyed when the chance came for them to move from their ghastly Poplar Avenue room – they had applied for assistance from the Memphis Housing Authority and were eventually rewarded with a dwelling place. This was at Lauderdale Courts, a federally funded housing project on Winchester Street intended for needy families with an income below a certain level. The rent was fixed by an Inspector whose job it was to judge how much each family could afford, and he assessed the rent for the Presley apartment at thirty-five dollars a month, which was also what their previous home had cost. An official check was made two or three times a year, firstly on the accommodation to ensure that it was not being abused, and secondly on the income of the breadwinner, who was not allowed to continue being subsidized if his income exceeded a prescribed limit.

Apartment 328, Lauderdale Courts, would be the Presley residence from 1949 until the first part of 1953. It consisted of a sitting-room, two bedrooms, a kitchen and a bathroom – some considerable improvement on their previous home despite its situation in the same run-down neighbourhood, in the vicinity of Humes High School and United Paint. Vernon's mother, Minnie Mae, had also moved into their Lauderdale Courts home, and every extra cent was welcome. In order to supplement the family income, Elvis began working as an usher at Loew's State Cinema on South Main Street, where he worked every evening from 5.00 p.m. until 10.00 p.m., for which he was paid twelve dollars seventy-five cents per week, although he only held the job for a few weeks, finding that it drastically detracted from his schoolwork. However, he returned to the cinema during the following summer, although once again his time as an employee of the picture house was brief – another usher reported to the manager that the popcorn girl was providing sweets

and popcorn on the sly to Elvis, who then attempted to remonstrate with the informer by punching him and was fired. Some time after this incident occurred, Elvis found himself another job. This one was at the Marl Metal Manufacturing Company (whose premises were on Georgia Avenue), where he earned one dollar per hour for working a shift lasting from 3.00 p.m. until 11.30 p.m. at night. This shift followed his school time each day, and it was thus hardly surprising that he began to suffer from severe exhaustion. When Vernon and Gladys learned that he had developed a tendency to fall asleep during his classes, they insisted that he resign the job. Later, Elvis found another source of income when his parents gave him enough money to buy a lawnmower and he began to charge neighbours for cutting their grass.

One reason why Elvis felt that he needed to work was the family's almost constant shortage of money, which was aggravated by both his parents needing to take time off due to ill health. As ever, it was his mother's example that no doubt provided the ultimate motivation, as Elvis later noted: 'We all worked hard – when my father hurt his back, my mother went to work on the wards in St. Joseph's hospital. She bathed patients, made beds, scrubbed floors and worked harder than ever before, and in the evening, she would come home and cook supper, do the housework and then mend other people's clothes.'

As a teenager Elvis seems not to have been a spendthrift, his major expenditure being on clothes and frequent excursions to local cinemas. In fact, the film world began to exert some influence on Elvis – although in a perfectly normal way. His screen idol was Tony Curtis, a Hollywood heart-throb who sported a distinctive (and at the time controversial) 'ducktail' haircut, a style Elvis himself adopted in the summer of 1951 after growing his hair longer. A touch of originality also saw him wearing prominent sideburns in tribute to a far less likely group of people whom he admired. 'Truck drivers were my idols', he later explained, 'and in Tupelo and Memphis, I'd see lots of truckers with sideburns, and it was my ambition at that time to look like them'. Elvis was in fact developing a 'new look' for himself, and

Elvis and his girlfriend, Dixie Locke, with Presley's cousin, Gene Smith, and his date, Betty, at the Humes High Prom in the early 1950s.

while he remained basically a shy person he was no longer the boy whom no one could remember. His new hairstyle set him apart from his contemporaries at school (most of whom favoured the 'All-American' crew-cut look), and his clothes were equally different. He had started to patronize a store on Memphis's celebrated Beale Street, close to the Mississippi river which dominates the city. 126 Beale Street was the site of Lansky Brothers, a shop which specialized in 'loud' clothes of the type particularly favoured by black entertainers. Their window display featured an eye-catching assortment of brightly coloured garments of various types – yellow suits, pink jackets, white shoes – which would in a few years help to create Elvis's first and most memorable image as a rock'n'roll star.

Although he continued to display a vital interest in music, this rarely, if ever, extended beyond listening and playing within the confines of his own home, and there is little evidence to suggest that he

seriously collaborated with other musicians until he embarked on a recording career. In addition, his musical preferences were not always of the type that his contemporaries shared – one particular example being his predilection for gospel music: 'When I was a child, I always wanted to be a member of a gospel quartet, and when I was sixteen years old, I went to the Ellis Auditorium in Memphis where they were holding an all-night gospel session. I had to go by myself, because none of the other kids of my age liked that kind of music. I saw the Blackwood Brothers Quartet and J. D. Sumner was a member of that group – I never dreamed that someday I'd be on the same stage as him.' (Nearly twenty years later, Sumner became a staple of Elvis's Las Vegas stage shows, although by then he led his own gospel group, J. D. Sumner & the Stamps.)

It was not so much that Elvis tried in any way to conceal his passion for music, but rather that very few people were aware that he sang and played guitar, as apparently he had few friends. Finally, someone who was more aware of his talent recommended Elvis to one of the teachers at his school, a Miss Scrivener, suggesting that he should be considered for a school concert that was coming up. Elvis later recalled his surprise: 'I thought that nobody knew I could sing, because I was very shy and I didn't consider myself that popular at school. I wasn't even dating anyone . . . Anyway, I came out and performed *Cold Cold Icy Fingers*, and when a student seemed to do well he was invited to do an encore. Miss Scrivener said "They like you – go out there and do another song", so I did – I sang *Till I Waltz With You Again*, and at the end, I heard this loud rumbling, which I suppose must have been applause. After it was all over, I said "They really did like me, didn't they, Miss Scrivener?" – I was amazed at how popular I became at school after that concert.'

According to his long-time associate Red West, the concert served as a kind of talent contest: 'He was an easy winner, but he seemed to be amazed that, for the first time in his life, someone other than his family really liked him, and it seemed as though he had finally found a way to make outsiders love him. As shy as he was, he had a definite magic on stage – whereas after the show he seemed to go back to being ordinary old Elvis, on stage he was in control.' This minor triumph was a rare escape into the world which he would soon bestride, and the only other documented public performance by Elvis during his years at school came when he sang and played in a show staged by a group of Humes students to entertain patients at the Memphis Veterans' Hospital.

The early summer of 1953 saw the eighteen-year-old Elvis leaving school. By this time, the Presley family had been forced to vacate their subsidized accommodation at Lauderdale Courts, as their joint income had increased to marginally exceed the limit allowed by the Memphis Housing Authority. Their new home was a smaller apartment, 398 Cypress Street, for which they had to pay an increased rent. The result was that the family stayed there only a few months, moving to Alabama Street (which was very close to Lauderdale Courts) where they lived in a larger apartment, at 462 Alabama Street, until the end of 1954. This was obviously an improvement on Cypress Street, although the rent was fifty dollars a month.

Elvis, having left school, had to find gainful employment, and his first full-time job was at the Precision Tool Company, where he was less than happy with the position, and soon moved on to the Crown Electrical Company. There, he was the youngest of the firm's employees and was (perhaps as a result) given the job of driving a Ford truck around Memphis delivering supplies. His boss, Mr. Tipler, later recalled that Elvis was a likeable young man – although slightly unusual-looking, because of his long hair. Tipler told Elvis's biographer, Jerry Hopkins, 'He went to the beautician to get his hair trimmed rather than to a regular barber. He was way ahead of the other fellows, even way back yonder'. His somewhat non-progressive position inspired Elvis to think about bettering his career prospects, but evenings spent studying to become an electrician do not seem to have given him a specific ambition to work in that field. 'When I was driving my truck and one of those shiny new cars went by, it started me dreaming. I always felt that someday something would change for me. I didn't know exactly what, but there was this feeling that the future looked kinda bright.' Not that a career as a professional musician was something about which he could do anything more than dream about at the time, although his battered old guitar accompanied him everywhere – even in the Ford truck which he drove around Memphis – in the hope that an opportunity to sing might arise: 'I used to go down to the fire station and sing to the boys there, because they were the only people who seemed to have time to listen!' His musical aspirations received little encouragement from his parents, as Elvis later said: 'My daddy knew a lot of guitar players, and most of them didn't work, and he said I must make up my mind to be either a guitar player or an electrician, but he also said that he'd never seen a guitar player that was worth a damn!'

Worship was still very much a part of the Presley family's activities, and they were part of the congregation of the First Assembly Of God Church at 1085

McLemore Avenue. (This street was later made famous by another notable musical act from Memphis, Booker T. & the MGs, who recorded instrumental versions of the songs on the Beatles' *Abbey Road* LP and titled their album *McLemore Avenue* after the street in which their recording studio was situated.) Another member of the church congregation was one of Elvis's first girlfriends, Dixie Locke, who noticed his keen interest in the R&B music he heard on the radio. Where previously black music and white music had been more or less mutually exclusive in radio programming terms, two pioneering local disc jockeys had been impressed by the growing enthusiasm among white kids for black music in the form of R&B, and were thus incorporating R&B records into their programme. Elvis certainly listened to both these progressive music lovers, Bill Gordon on station WMPS, and Dewey Phillips, whose show was known as 'Red Hot and Blue', on WHBQ, but he also tuned in to a local black-owned and -staffed station, WDIA, among whose disc jockeys were two musicians who would later become much more famous: soul star Rufus Thomas and supreme blues guitarist Riley 'B.B.' King. Both had made records at a small studio on Union Avenue run almost single-handedly by Sam Phillips.

Sam was born in 1923 on a farm near Florence, Alabama, and had loved black music since his childhood days. Following the death of his father (during the early part of the Second World War), he was forced to leave High School to support his mother and aunt. His work as master of ceremonies at a summer concert impressed a radio executive from Muscle Shoals, Alabama, and Sam was invited to join the executive's station, WLAY, as a disc jockey in 1942. Phillips moved around various radio stations in the South, before joining a Memphis station, WREC, in 1946. By 1950, he had saved enough money to indulge one of his fantasies and set up his own recording studio (his radio career having also provided him with a knowledge of the rudiments of studio engineering). It was nevertheless a brave decision to leave the comparative security of the airways to set up the 'Memphis Recording Service', as Phillips called his enterprise. He found a

suitable building for his premises at 706 Union Avenue, near Beale Street and close to several used car lots, and opened a studio which, he claimed, offered 'a complete service to fill every recording need'.

He swiftly found himself in demand to make recordings of various local social functions – not at all what he had in mind when he conceived the idea of the studio. Rather, Phillips wanted the main thrust of the studio to be in recording the black blues and R&B artists whose music he loved, but who were being ignored by the major white-dominated record companies and as a result being released on a number of enterprising independent labels, including Specialty, which operated from Los Angeles; Chess, from Chicago; and Atlantic, from New York. Even so, the resources of these companies during the early 1950s were not sufficient to allow nationwide coverage by talent scouts, and Phillips realized that Memphis, despite its plethora of talented musicians, was being overlooked even by the independent companies: local musicians were rarely if ever given the opportunity to make records. Phillips later explained, 'It seemed to me that Negroes were the only people who had any frankness left in their music, and there was no place in the South where they could go to record. The nearest place was Chicago, and most of the musicians in Memphis didn't have the money or the time to make the trip. [After I opened] Gradually the word got around Beale Street that there was a studio in town which wouldn't rip people off.'

Between 1950 and 1952, Sam recorded a number of great R&B artists who were finding it difficult to record elsewhere, and leased the completed masters to companies like Modern and RPM in Los Angeles and Chess/Checker in Chicago. Among those he cut were B. B. King, Howlin' Wolf, 'Big' Walter Horton, Joe Hill Louis and Rosco Gordon, plus several acts brought to him by a local studio musician, Ike Turner (who later achieved fame in the company of his wife Tina). One of Turner's discoveries was Jackie Brenston, whose *Rocket 88* was probably the biggest record made in Phillips's studios in their early days. By the end of 1952, however, things were not quite the way Phillips had expected, for many of the artists whom he had helped to

launch had left Memphis and headed for Chicago (where they found immediate access to Chess Records) while Modern/RPM, noticing how fruitful the Memphis Recording Service had been in fostering new talent, had established their own recording studio in another part of the city. The obvious solution was for Sam Phillips to start his own label, and he formed Sun Records in partnership with his brother Judd. A commercial artist was engaged to design a suitable logo for the new label, and the result – a crowing rooster silhouetted by a red and yellow sunset along with a few musical notes – became world-famous.

The first Sun record was scheduled to be *Blues In My Condition* by Jackie Boy (a pre-war bluesman named Jack Kelly) and Little Walter (in fact, 'Big' Walter Horton), but an adverse radio reaction to advance pressings led to it being withdrawn, and the following month, March 1952, saw the first Sun record available in record stores. This was Johnny London's *Drivin' Slow*. It was not a hit, and nor was another concurrent release by Walter Bradford and the Big City Four, with the result that the label was suspended for a year, until the following March, by which time its artist roster contained several better-known local names like Joe Hill Louis and Willie Nix. Finally, the eighth single released on Sun became a hit – ironically, in view of what would later occur, it was in the form of an 'answer' record to a hit by Willie Mae 'Big Mama' Thornton titled *Hound Dog*, written by a pair of young New Yorkers, Jerry Leiber and Mike Stoller, which Presley himself later recorded after coming to fame. Sun's 'answer' was *Bear Cat* by Rufus Thomas, which reached the national R&B charts before legal action was taken by the record company that had released *Hound Dog* for infringement of copyright. By this time, however, Sun and Sam Phillips had the scent of success in their nostrils, and releases (and, to a certain extent, hits) arrived with greater regularity. Among the more notable Sun releases of this period, three seem particularly interesting – Little Junior Parker's *Mystery Train* (which Presley later recorded); *Just Walkin' In The Rain* by the Prisonaires, a group of convicted criminals incarcerated in the Tennessee State Penitentiary in Nashville, but whose song was later taken to the top of the world's charts by the redoubtable Johnny Ray, a superstar of the 1950s; and the most obscure of the three, *My Kind Of Carryin' On* by Doug Poindexter and the Starlite Wranglers. This record marked the recording debut of a young guitarist named Winfield Scott Moore, who would shortly afterwards feature in the early career of a young truck driver from Memphis named Elvis.

'Scotty' Moore had served in the U.S. Navy and later worked first as a mechanic and then as a hatter, along the way teaching himself to play the guitar at the instigation of his father and three brothers, who could all play musical instruments. His work in the hat department of this brother's clothes-cleaning plant allowed him time to spend most afternoons trying to further his musical aspirations, and in the course of his travels he inevitably became aware of Sam Phillips and the Memphis Recording Service, largely as a result of joining the Starlite Wranglers, a strictly country and western group whose music was strongly influenced by Poindexter's hero, Hank Williams, who had died tragically a few months before. Another Starlite Wrangler was bass player Bill Black, who would also soon see his life changing as a result of meeting Elvis Presley. At the time they backed Poindexter in Sam Phillips's studios, however, they had certainly never heard Presley's name.

THE HILLBILLY CAT

Some time between June and October 1953, Elvis visited the small one-storey Sun Records building at 706 Union Avenue, Memphis. He knew of Sam Phillips's reputation as a record producer and had heard several of the records made at Sun, first with bluesmen and later with young white hillbilly singers, thus the visit was almost certainly undertaken in the hope that he would be able to audition for Phillips and for the record label. However, Phillips was out when Elvis arrived, so he talked instead to Marion Keisker, Phillips's secretary, who recalled, 'He said he was a singer, so I asked him what kind of singer he was, and he told me he could sing any kind of music. I said "Do you sing hillbilly?" and he said he could, so I asked him again who he sounded like in hillbilly, and he told me the same thing, that he could sound like anybody'.

As well as Sun Records, Sam Phillips also ran the Memphis Recording Service, which offered facilities for cutting single one-sided acetates at a cost of four dollars. This service was used by a variety of people wishing to record anything from poetry to speeches, but Elvis asked if he could record two songs as a birthday gift for his mother. Taken at face value this was a rather strange request, since Gladys Presley's birthday had been two months or more earlier, in April. Also, the family had not yet acquired a record player, and it would have been easier and cheaper anyway to make such a disc in one of the booths at a Memphis department store. In fact, although Elvis had every intention of giving the record to his mother, his major objective was to be heard singing by a representative of the Sun label.

He performed *My Happiness*, a song made famous by the Ink Spots (a popular black vocal group), and *That's When Your Heartaches Begin*, a country ballad. Normally, such a recording would have been cut straight on to the acetate, which would have been the only copy of the performance. On this occasion, however, Marion Keisker did something unusual – impressed by his style, she taped part of the recording. 'I grabbed this old crumpled piece of tape laying on the counter and ran it through the tape machine real quick', she remembers. The result was that she managed to record the final part of *My Happiness* and all of *That's When Your Heartaches Begin*. Asked later why she made an exception to the usual procedure in the case of Elvis, Marion explained: 'Over and over, I remember Sam saying, "If I could find a white man who had a Negro sound and the Negro feel I could make a billion dollars", and that was what I heard in Elvis, that . . . what I guess they now call "soul", that Negro sound, so I taped it, because I wanted Sam to know.' Marion put a note with the tape – 'Elvis Presley. Good ballad singer. 462 Alabama Street. 375 630. Hold.' As the Presley family were not on the telephone, the number given belonged the Frutcher family, who lived upstairs.

Sam Phillips apparently listened to the tape when he returned to the office, and was to some extent impressed, although he did nothing immediately in terms of contacting Elvis – at that point, he clearly saw no connection between the eighteen-year-old singer and his billion-dollar ambitions. Seemingly even Elvis himself thought little of his first record, which he compared to 'someone banging a trash can lid', although his mother was very pleased. 'She borrowed a record player and played it over and over until it was plumb wore out', Elvis recalled – acetates of this

Opposite: *One of the earliest photographs of Elvis the professional musician.*

inexpensive type were of poor quality, and would inevitably have worn out after a short time, so Elvis Presley's historic first recording no longer exists. The record was doubtless thrown away when it became unplayable, or else was lost – a fate that also befell the piece of tape which Marion Keisker had used to capture the latter part of his performance.

Around the same time, Elvis was becoming involved with other singers and musicians, although on a friendly basis rather than as a fellow-performer. He was still very keen to become a gospel singer, and had met members of the Songfellows, the junior branch of the Blackwood Brothers Quartet, at all-night gospel sessions in Memphis and at a live lunchtime radio show, 'High Noon Roundup', broadcast by a local station, WMPS, and hosted by a popular local disc-jockey, Bob Neal, who would later play an important role in furthering Elvis's career. In fact, his friendship with the Songfellows might have led to a first professional opportunity for Elvis, as one

of the members was planning to leave the group towards the end of 1953, and Elvis was asked whether he might be interested in becoming the singer's replacement. He was most enthusiastic, of course, but later the singer changed his mind about leaving, with the result that the vacancy obviously no longer existed.

On January 4, 1954 (several months after his first visit), Elvis returned to Union Avenue, where he found that while Marion Keisker was absent, Sam Phillips was available. It seems probable that Elvis had called to discover whether Marion had convinced Phillips of his potential, but as she was away, Elvis decided that the best approach was to cut another four dollar record. This second recording comprised a ballad, *Casual Love*, and a country song, *I'll Never Stand In Your Way*. Once again, a note was taken of Elvis's name and telephone number, and Phillips indicated that he might call Elvis should any singing opportunities arise.

Over the next few weeks, Marion would periodically remind her boss of Elvis when something needed to be recorded and no singer was immediately available. Her suggestion was finally heeded when a demonstration record of a song titled *Without You* arrived from a Nashville publishing company. 'It was a single voice with a single guitar, a simple, lovely ballad,' Marion told Jerry Hopkins. 'Sam couldn't find out who the singer was – he was told it was a Negro kid who was hanging round the studio when the song came in, so he said: "If I can't find that kid I'll have to find someone else, because I want to release that song." So I told Sam, "What about the kid with the sideburns?"' Phillips maintained that he had no idea of how to get in touch with Elvis – whose name he had already forgotten – but fortunately Marion recalled taking the telephone number of the Presleys' neighbours, whom she then called. (According to legend, Elvis drove the fifteen blocks from his home to the Sun studio at breakneck speed, to the point where Marion was still holding the telephone when he arrived!)

Elvis listened to the song and then sang it, but his performance was, by all accounts, awful. Further attempts showed little improvement, and in despair Sam Phillips asked Elvis what else he could do. 'I can do anything', replied Elvis confidently, so Phillips suggested that he give an immediate demonstration. According to Marion Keisker, 'He started playing snatches of anything he knew – religious, gospel, western, everything, but real heavy on the Dean Martin stuff. Apparently, he'd decided that if he was going to sound like anybody else, it was going to be like Dean Martin.' Martin was in fact a reasonably good choice to ape, as he was enjoying stardom both in films (in humorous partnership with Jerry Lewis), and on record with a series of big hits on both sides of the Atlantic which, although they had little to do with the type of music for which Presley would become famous, were nevertheless substantial sellers.

Phillips was impressed, but could tell that the young singer was extremely inexperienced and needed to work with other musicians, and so pronounced that he would try to find a band with whom Elvis could work. Shortly afterwards, he mentioned Elvis to Scotty Moore. Scotty used to visit the Sun studios after finishing work in the hat department of his brother's company, in the hope of finding some musical endeavour that might use his ability as a guitar player, and he and Sam Phillips would usually adjourn to Miss Taylor's Restaurant, next door to the cramped Sun offices. Phillips frequently used the restaurant for meetings (almost invariably choosing the third booth by the window), and he and Scotty would discuss music over cups of coffee – they had similar musical tastes and ambitions of 'making it' in the music business, although neither was quite clear about the way to achieve their aims. 'We were all looking for something,' Moore remembers, 'although we didn't know quite what it was, (but we wanted) just some way to get through the door. One day, he mentioned this kid who had come in to make a record and had a real good voice, so every day for two solid weeks I'd go down there in the afternoon and ask him if he'd called this guy Elvis, and he'd say "No, I haven't done it yet". I think Marion heard us talking and she finally went and dug through the files, pulled out the card and said, "Here – call!"'

Scotty then telephoned Elvis, announcing himself as a representative of Sun Records, and inviting the young man to his house, while Bill Black, who had played bass with Scotty in the Starlite Wranglers, and lived close by, was also invited. Elvis's appearance came as something of a surprise, according to Scotty: 'He was wearing a pink suit, white shoes and a ducktail [hairstyle], and I thought my wife was going to go out the back door! We sat around for a couple of hours and went through a little bit of everything – Marty Robbins, Billy Eckstine, you name it . . .' The collaboration obviously showed promise, and Scotty told Sam Phillips on the following day: 'The boy sings fine – with the right song and the right backing, who knows?' Phillips thereupon encouraged him to rehearse with Elvis and Bill Black, and some weeks later, the trio assembled in the Sun studio with a view to trying to make a record. The date of the session – July 5, 1954 – happened to be one of the hottest evenings of the year.

In the hot humid atmosphere of the small 12 foot by 12 foot studio, the trio played some of the tunes they had practised, with Sam Phillips listening in the control booth. The first song to be recorded was the country ballad *I Love You Because*, originally a hit in 1949 for Leon Payne who had also written the song, but the slow mournful performance by Elvis was not to Sam Phillips's taste, and in fact, the song remained unreleased until after RCA Records assumed ownership (in late 1955) of all the Presley masters recorded for Sun. Several other songs were also tried, but without any greater success, at which point a break was called in the session, and the musicians relaxed with cold drinks to chat. Suddenly, Elvis started singing a blues written by one of his favourite black performers, Arthur 'Big Boy' Crudup, *That's All Right*, which Crudup had originally recorded in 1946. Scotty Moore takes up the story: 'It was an accident, really – Elvis started singing and was clowning and jumping all over the studio, and Bill picked up his bass and started slapping it, getting a rhythm going. Not wanting to be left out, I grabbed my guitar and started trying to find something to play along with, and then Sam came to the studio door and asked what we were doing, and we said we didn't know. He said "Well, it sounds pretty good through the door – go back to the microphones and see if you can do it again", so we looked at each other as if to say, "You must be kidding". Then we struggled around for a minute or two, figured out a musical formula, ran through it a couple of times, I think, and then recorded it.'

This version of *That's All Right* was neither blues, like the original, nor country, like the songs they had previously recorded – it was a mixture of styles, but with something extra, the result being fast blues with a country beat, which Sam Phillips found both exhilarating and exciting. Elvis sounded breathless and on the verge of losing control, Bill Black slapped the strings of his double bass, Scotty made his guitar ring, and Phillips combined the whole into a powerful echo-laden production.

The resulting record became a rock'n' roll classic. The sound, which was original and unfamiliar at the time, seems less remarkable today only because so many others have copied or been influenced by it, something which is particularly true of

Scotty Moore's guitar sound, about which he has been questioned on many subsequent occasions, but without being able to provide a full explanation, simply because it was not something he had planned. 'It's a combination of several styles rolled into one,' he averred a quarter of a century later. 'I was a big fan of Merle Travis and Chet Atkins (both highly rated country music guitarists) and also a lot of blues players. I didn't go looking for an original sound, but because we were only a trio, I had to do more than I'd been used to in a band. I had to develop a combination of rhythm plus a few notes – you could say I was forced into it.'

Sam Phillips's contribution to the sound was to use what Scotty calls 'tape slap' to give the track its echo effect: 'He was the first to really capitalize on that sound to enhance the recording of music', notes Scotty. 'It had been used before that for the movies, but not on records.' Moore went on to use an amplifier which produced a similar sound during live performances, the delaying effect and fuller sound being achieved by a recording head from a tape machine, which intercepted the sound of the guitar.

Although the recording of *That's All Right* should certainly be termed historic, it cannot be said to mark the start of rock'n'roll on record. Other performers had previously combined black and white styles of music successfully – the track's enormous importance and influence was because Elvis was to become the biggest pop star of all, initiating the musical revolution spearheaded by rock'n'roll that gave teenagers of the post-war era a subculture and sound of their own. John Lennon, one of the handful of rock stars whose influence has ever threatened to exceed that of Presley, spoke for millions of teenagers who grew up in the late 1950s when he said that nothing had really affected him before he heard Elvis.

However, Presley's incredible success was still more than eighteen months away when he recorded *That's All Right*, and the musicians can have had little idea of just how significant their first recording session together would become, although Sam Phillips may have had an inkling, as it was he who had recognized the spark in the frivolity during the studio break and insisted that it be repeated and recorded, despite the attitude of the musicians that it was of little consequence.

The following evening saw the four men back in the studio attempting to record another song which could be used as the second side of the debut single by Elvis, and although it seemed that a magic formula had been discovered for *That's All Right*, they found themselves unable to immediately apply it to other material. Several other tunes were tried, including a version of Bill Monroe's bluegrass classic, *Blue Moon Of Kentucky*. Alternate takes from this session reveal that Elvis at first tried to perform the song in the ballad style he strongly favoured, but after another break in recording, the trio arrived at the up-tempo version which was eventually released. 'Bill Black started it', remembers Scotty Moore. 'He was straddled across his bass, and for some reason he started singing *Blue Moon Of Kentucky* and clowning around. Elvis started playing rhythm guitar with him, and we just jived it up.' Sam Phillips was very pleased with this new arrangement, and when the recording was finished, said 'Fine, man – hell, that's different, that's a pop song now'. He quickly set about preparing the two songs for release as a single with a catalogue number of SUN 209.

The next step was to try to ensure that the record was played on the radio, which was as important in 1954 as it is today – without radio exposure, a record would not be heard, and thus would be unlikely to sell – and Phillips realized that its uncategorizable nature might lead to problems concerning the launch of Elvis's recording career. The record was neither country nor R&B, and was likely to sound too 'pop' for country stations yet too country flavoured for black outlets.

After playing the record to several disc jockey friends, whose reaction was generally favourable, although none would risk programming it, Phillips approached the one man he was fairly sure would be sufficiently adventurous to play it, Dewey Phillips (no relation), who hosted a show titled 'Red Hot And Blue' on station WHBQ, Memphis. Dewey, like Alan Freed of WJW, Cleveland, Ohio (and later of WINS, New York City), was one of the pioneering American disc jockeys who realized that white teenagers wanted their own music as distinct from

that enjoyed by their parents. Black R&B was proving particularly popular among young white kids, who enjoyed the music despite (or perhaps because of) the disapproval of their elders. Elvis himself was no exception, once saying: 'I dug the real low-down Mississippi singers, mostly Big Bill Broonzy and "Big Boy" Crudup, although they would scold me at home for listening to them. "Sinful music" the townsfolk of Memphis said it was, which never bothered me, I guess.'

Dewey Phillips had a strong empathy with the hip teenagers of the city, and kept a telephone close at hand when he was on the air to facilitate direct contact with his listeners. When he played an acetate of the first recordings by Elvis, he was immediately inundated with calls enquiring about the singer – one night, audience response is said to have amounted to forty-seven telephone requests for Elvis, plus fourteen telegrams on the same subject. Wink Martindale, now a radio personality in Los Angeles, was an announcer at WHBQ, and recalled 'Dewey just kept flipping the record over, playing one side after the other all night long'.

Elvis himself didn't hear that show, as he was at the Suzore No. 2 theatre in downtown Memphis watching a cowboy film, but Dewey Phillips contacted Vernon Presley and asked him to bring his son to the radio station for an interview. After Vernon and Gladys had found him and taken him to WHBQ, Elvis was excited, but also very nervous – 'Mr. Phillips, I don't know nothing about being interviewed', to which Dewey replied, 'Just don't say nothing dirty', before playing Elvis's record, after which he began to ask questions. One concerned the school Elvis had attended, the all-white Humes High – Dewey later noted: 'I wanted to get that out, because a lot of people listening thought he was coloured'. After several minutes of chatting, Phillips thanked Elvis for talking to him, at which Elvis said, 'Aren't you going to interview me?', and was then shocked to discover that the microphone had been open all the time. He had been under the impression that what had taken place was a warm-up for the real thing. 'He broke out into a cold sweat', reported Dewey.

Soon afterwards, the record was played

on WMPS, a Memphis country music station, thanks to a disc jockey known as Uncle Richard, while shops began to order the disc from Sun. Sam Phillips officially released it on July 19, deliberately neglecting to nominate an A side, in the hope that radio stations that found one side of the record unacceptable might try the other.

Meanwhile, Elvis was becoming a minor celebrity in Memphis, and was interviewed on July 27 by Edwin Howard, of the 'Memphis Press-Scimitar'. The five-paragraph story that appeared the following day contained no quotes from Elvis, who had been so nervous that he could only manage deferential 'No sir''s and 'Yes sir''s in response to questions, while Marion Keisker had done most of the talking, being quoted as saying of the record: 'The odd thing about it is that both sides seem to be equally popular on pop, country and race record shows. This boy has something that seems to appeal to everybody. We've only just gotten sample records out to the disc jockeys and distributors, but we got big orders yesterday from Dallas and Atlanta.'

By this time, Elvis, Scotty and Bill had begun performing in Memphis, as Scotty Moore recalled 'At first, there was some thought of making Elvis part of our other group, the Starlite Wranglers, but that didn't last long, and shortly after that, the group disbanded'. Elvis was billed for a time as the 'hillbilly cat'. Scotty explained: 'The 'cat' was going to the R&B side, and the 'hillbilly' was country, of course – we were technically playing country music, but it didn't come out that way!'

Elvis had yet to perfect the controversial stage movements that would provoke adulation among teenagers and anger among adults – 'He wasn't really that set on himself in those days,' notes Scotty. 'It was Bill who was the clown, riding that double bass and generally cutting up, which stemmed from a lot of country acts using the bass that way. But as time went by, Elvis worked into a kind of routine – he may not have known what he wanted at first, but when he figured it out, he got it to them.'

Predictably, several local businessmen became interested in directing Elvis's career, but Sam Phillips suggested that

Scotty Moore should act as manager until the singer's direction and development became clearer, by which time someone who could do the job honestly and professionally would have been found, and on July 12, 1954, Moore became Elvis's first manager. The simple one-page contract which they signed stated:

'It is agreed that W. S. Moore III will take over the complete management and professional affairs of the said Elvis Presley, book him professionally for all appearances that can be secured for him, and promote him generally in all his general endeavours. The said W. S. Moore III is to receive as compensation for his services ten per cent (10%) of all earnings from engagements, appearances and bookings made by him for Elvis Presley.'

The contract was also signed by Vernon and Gladys Presley, as Elvis was still under 21 years of age, and the result was that Scotty took an initial ten per cent, after which the rest of the trio's income was divided three ways, Elvis taking half, and Scotty and Bill splitting equally the remaining half.

At the end of July 1954, they were booked to appear on a country package show headlined by Slim Whitman, Webb Pierce and Marty Robbins at the Overton Park Shell in Memphis, which was the first time they had played before a large audience. It was also significant as the first occasion on which Elvis displayed his infamous 'wiggle' – in a 1956 interview published in 'T.V. Guide', he recalled the concert and its aftermath: 'I was scared stiff – it was my first big appearance in front of an audience. I came out and was doing a fast type tune, and everybody was hollering, but I didn't know what they were hollering at. When I came off stage, my manager told me they were hollering because I was wiggling! Well, I went back for an encore, and I kinda did a little more, and the more I did, the wilder they got.' Webb Pierce has a slightly different explanation for the first wiggle, remembering Elvis saying that he was afraid he might faint in the heat, so that he had begun to flap his legs to guard against passing out, but whatever the reason, the wiggling had a dramatic effect. While this may seem surprising, since most of today's rock acts move around during their performance, prior to Elvis most pop stars tended to stand still, rarely moving any parts of their body save their heads and occasionally their arms. Another version of the origin of the 'wiggle' has been provided by Sam Phillips: 'The audience hadn't warmed up to him as much as we'd hoped – he looked cramped when he sang, and when he came offstage, I told him "You've really got to move". I suggested he square off against the mike and shake his head up and down. Well, he went back out there and it was as though he'd released all the tension. That left leg of his really took off!'

After that first major concert, life for Elvis became even more hectic – as well as playing more and more live dates around Memphis, he still had his day job at Crown Electric, and was also preparing for his next single. The first record had done well locally, but made little impact elsewhere, although the nationally distributed music trade magazine 'Billboard' had praised Elvis as, 'a potent new chanter who can sock over a tune for either the country or R&B markets'. Sam Phillips had worked hard on promoting the record, concentrating all his resources on Elvis and temporarily abandoning his other acts, but Sun's status as a small independent label meant that it had only patchy distribution arrangements outside the Memphis area, while Elvis, Scotty and Bill still had day jobs, which prevented them embarking on extensive promotional tours.

Nevertheless, Phillips had important contacts with the Grand Ole Opry in Nashville – a live radio show which was broadcast from this auditorium over a powerful 'clear channel' from station WSM, Nashville, attracting an audience of several million in the American South and Midwest. Phillips arranged for Elvis to appear at the Opry on September 25, 1954, coinciding with the release of his second single, which again coupled blues, *Good Rockin' Tonight*, and a country song, *I Don't Care If The Sun Don't Shine*, with both tracks performed in the energetic rockabilly style that had characterized his debut. However, the prestigious appearance turned out to be less successful than Sam had planned, as the show's booker, Jim Denny, only allowed Elvis to perform the two tracks on his first record,

and was also upset to discover that the backing group comprised only two musicians, angrily asking: 'Where are the rest of the band?' Marion Keisker, who was at the show, recalled: 'One of the great mysteries that perplexed everyone was how Sam got that sound – it was such a big sound that everybody thought there was a big band on the record, and Jim Denny thought he was getting at least four or five people besides Elvis'.

The Grand Ole Opry, which dates back to the 1920s, is a country music institution. Elvis had listened to the show as a child, building up a mental picture of this 'shrine' (in reality, the Ryman Auditorium in downtown Nashville) which far

exceeded fact – 'You mean this is what I've been dreaming about all these years?' he asked Marion Keisker, gazing at the solemn, rather drab building that had changed little since its construction in 1892 as a religious tabernacle. The reaction to his performance was equally disappointing, since the Opry audience were somewhat staid and conservative in their musical tastes, and Jim Denny compounded the disapproval by suggesting that Elvis should return to driving trucks. The latter was deeply hurt, and remembered years later, 'That broke my heart', although it should be noted in Denny's defence that his dismissive attitude to Elvis was one of only a few mistakes he made in a lengthy career – among other things, he played an important role in the acquisition of Buddy Holly's first recording contract, even if he was completely wrong about the potential displayed by Elvis.

Despite this cool reception, Sam Phillips was able to book Elvis for another important radio show, the 'Louisiana Hayride', which was aired each Saturday night from Shreveport, Louisiana, and was second only to the Opry in terms of prestige among country music fans, while adopting a less conservative musical outlook. Its reputation as a 'cradle of the stars' had been earned by assisting the fledgling careers of such notable artists as Hank Williams, Webb Pierce and Slim Whitman, and would have a similar effect with Elvis Presley, who made his debut on the 'Hayride' on October 16, 1954. He was introduced by booker/announcer Frank Page, who said: 'Just a few weeks ago, a young man from Memphis, Tennessee, recorded a song on the Sun label, and in just a matter of weeks, that record has skyrocketed up the charts, and it's really doing well all over the country. He's only 19 years old, he's a singer who's forging a new style – Elvis Presley!' After noting the good reaction from the audience, Page invited Elvis back, eventually signing him to a one-year contract to appear regularly on the 'Hayride'.

Page later recalled 'He filled it up every Saturday night. Usually, some of the 3500 seats were empty, but not with Elvis there'. Scotty Moore also saw the Hayride shows as significant: 'I think that was where we knew things were starting to happen. He had a large audience, and it was quite obvious that they were very receptive to what he was doing – they loved it, and he could work an audience to death'.

In November 1954, Elvis left his job at Crown Electric to concentrate full time on a singing career, and soon afterwards, engaged another musician for live work in the shape of drummer D. J. Fontana, a regular on the 'Louisiana Hayride'. For recording, however, the original trio of Elvis, Scotty and Bill was not augmented, and they returned to the Sun studio in December to record a third single, *You're A Heartbreaker*. It was a slow country number but, as usual, somewhat supercharged, although with a modicum of restraint, but with *Milkcow Blues Boogie*, a blues of 1930 vintage, the musicians began playing slowly, and were then interrupted by Elvis, who drawls, 'Hold it, fellas – that don't move me. Let's get real, real gone', before launching into a considerably faster, funkier version of the tune. This technique of creating an almost artificial excitement had been used by musicians for many years, and while it has never been clear who conceived the 'false start' idea, it seems that recording with Elvis during his earliest days was rarely a straightforward matter, as Marion Keisker told Jerry Hopkins: 'Every session came hard, and he wasn't like Johnny Cash and the ones who came later who had their material prepared and were always ready to record. First thing (with Elvis), he'd want to record something he'd heard on the jukebox, and Sam would have to persuade him that he couldn't do that'.

Elvis with Red West (second left) and some other friends, 1956.

Elvis still liked the idea of singing slow mournful songs, but Sam preferred faster, rockabilly material – years later, Elvis would have great success with ballads, although he was only able to persuade Sam Phillips to record a handful, notably *I Love You Because* and the atmospheric *Blue Moon*, which were not commercially released until they were acquired, along with Elvis's recording contract, by RCA Records.

The third single sold fairly well around Memphis, but emulated its predecessors by achieving little elsewhere, confirming the impression that Elvis's career was not progressing as might have been expected. One possible explanation for the lack of progress was that Scotty Moore was finding it increasingly difficult to combine the duties of manager and guitarist – as he said later, 'I was interested in playing, not booking shows and telling people how to sing'.

Early in 1955 Scotty was pleased and relieved to be replaced as manager by Bob Neal (real name Robert Neal Hopgood), who was well known on the Memphis music scene as a popular disc jockey on WMPS, but who also organized country shows and ran a local record shop. Red West, Elvis's schoolfriend who began travelling with the musicians to shows in 1955, described Neal as 'a real good ole boy, a straight shooter. He seemed to be more in for the fun than the money – he was a pretty funny dude, who might have made it as a stand up comic if he'd worked at it'. Neal booked Elvis and the Blue Moon Boys (as he renamed Scotty, Bill and D.J.) on the school-house circuit, advertising their dates on his radio show and opening concerts by telling elderly jokes and playing a ukelele. There were occasions when more people would come to see Neal than his protégés – some audiences didn't take to Elvis, due to his wild behaviour on stage and his outrageous clothing, pink and black being his preferred combination of colours, but as the year progressed, he was becoming an increasingly big attraction, and very much the star of the show. Also, the financial arrangements altered accordingly, with Scotty, Bill and D.J. receiving salaries

On stage, 1956. Left to right, Elvis, Scotty Moore (partly obscured), D.J. Fontana and Bill Black.

rather than percentages, Bob Neal taking fifteen per cent as a management fee, and a further ten per cent of Elvis's income going towards promotion.

Meanwhile, Elvis's mother, although pleased at the success her son was achieving, was worried both about the amount of travelling he was undertaking and the sometimes over-enthusiastic attention of fans – Scotty Moore recalled: 'Every time we'd go out, Gladys Presley would call either Bill or myself, saying, "You be sure and take care of my boy".' However, Elvis had not forgotten his parents, and whenever he was out of town for the night, he would call his mother, and although he wasn't earning fortunes in 1955, he gave Vernon and Gladys what he could – his mother continued to take occasional jobs despite frequent illness, while his father was still working for the United Paint Company, despite a long period away from work due to back trouble, which made financial contributions from Elvis particularly welcome – where other young men might have been more interested only in their own acquisitions, Elvis was always concerned about providing for his parents.

Despite his growing fame (or perhaps because of it) Elvis still had few close associates – Scotty and Co. were his friends on the road, of course, but otherwise his closest companion was his girlfriend, Dixie Locke, with whom he 'went steady' for almost two years until the end of 1955, carrying her picture in a compartment of his wrist watch. 'In all the time we were together', she remembered, 'he didn't have anyone I would call friends, except his cousins, although there were school-type chums that just dropped in, came and went, so to speak. But no one else was really that close to him – I think I'd have known about them if there had been.'

There was a still marked contrast between the on-stage and off-stage Elvis – as a performer, he was wilder and more energetic than any singer most of his audiences had previously experienced, but in his private life he was still very quiet and polite, apart from the enjoyment he gained from clowning with his musician friends, which included playing practical jokes on them, especially when they were trying to sleep. Scotty remembers: 'He

had so much nervous energy we had to sit up nights to wear him out so that we could sleep'. D. J. Fontana tells similar stories: 'We had to pull all sorts of tricks on him so that we could get to sleep' – Elvis's problems with sleeping were to increase as his career developed, and led him eventually to resort to drugs to help him sleep, although the result was that he also needed drugs to help him wake up.

Another problem relating to his increasing fame was the jealousy displayed by boyfriends of the girls who screamed and swooned at Elvis's concerts. While Elvis could certainly stand up for himself in a one-to-one confrontation, there were fears for his safety after shows, which was the reason for Red West travelling with the band, as protection for the star from jealous men and over-excited fans. Red recounted in 'Elvis: What Happened?', 'When I saw those chicks leaping up onstage trying to kiss him, I knew we were in for some old-fashioned battles. I could see the faces of some of those boyfriends sitting there while their girls went crazy about Elvis, and man, they were as black as thunder'. At the end of a concert in Florida, fans got onto the stage and began to tear at Elvis's clothes, and Red noted, 'It looked like they were trying to eat him all up, tearing and clawing like animals. One of the legs of his pants went, then his shirt was torn to shreds. We managed to get him off the stage, but in shreds'.

As Presley's fame grew, music-business entrepreneurs became increasingly interested, among them the self-styled 'Colonel' Tom Parker, who had managed the successful careers of artists Eddy Arnold and Hank Snow. After watching Elvis's progress with interest, Parker became involved more closely when he helped Bob Neal book the singer for a concert in Carlsbad, New Mexico, and the more he heard of this rising star, the greater his interest became. Elvis was never the headline attraction when he performed with country artists. He invariably went on stage last, as the audience became so wound up by his act that he was almost impossible to follow and anyone else seemed comparatively tame and dull. Despite his increasing interest, Parker took some time before getting heavily involved with Elvis, staying in the background and seeking the opinions of those who worked with Elvis, like country entertainer Whitey Ford, known as 'The Duke Of Paducah', who was on a tour that Parker organized featuring Hank Snow and Mother Maybelle and the Carter Family. Parker's enthusiasm increased by leaps and bounds after the release of the fourth Sun single, *Baby Let's Play House/I'm Left, You're Right, She's Gone*, which sold considerably more than the previous three, and entered the national country charts on July 6, 1955, eventually reaching the Top Ten, and remaining on the chart for fifteen weeks. It was at this point that Parker decided that he should manage Elvis, to which end he began to gear himself up to take over – he was forty-six years old, a chubby balding man with a reputation as a shrewd and crafty businessman, who had worked with carnivals and circuses prior to moving into music, where he handled country artists.

Parker's origins seem somewhat mysterious – he claimed to have been born on June 26, 1909, in Huntington, West Virginia, but Presley biographer Albert Goldman has recently asserted that although the date was correct, Parker's actual birthplace was the city of Breda in Holland, and that his real name is Andreas Cornelis van Kuijk (known to his family as Andre). One of nine children, he was born above a stable and his father, who had been a soldier for many years, was skilled with horses. His mother was of French ancestry, her family having travelled with a carnival. As a result, young Andre enjoyed equestrian pursuits as a child, showing a particular facination for the circus, while he is also apparently remembered for his ability to convince people that he should be paid to run errands. At the age of eighteen, he embarked on the long trip to the United States by ship, returning to Holland a year later with presents for all his family, before leaving again several months later. In 1930, after his family heard that he had joined the U.S. Army, they began to receive letters and money on a regular basis, although these were signed 'Tom Parker' rather than Andre van Kuijk. The letters stopped at the beginning of 1932, and the family heard nothing more until 1961, when he was recognized in a newspaper photograph with Elvis. Although it had been almost thirty years since anyone

had seen him, he was instantly recognizable as he looked just like his brother!

It appears that after leaving the Army, Parker became involved with a circus. America was in the midst of the Great Depression, and Parker would have needed all his legendary financial acumen to earn much money, although years later, he delighted in recounting tales of the blatant tricks he employed, including painting sparrows yellow in order to pass them off as canaries, selling 'foot-long' hot dogs that contained only small pieces of meat at each end of a long roll, and the celebrated 'dancing chickens', who were encouraged to live up to their billing by the electric hot plate that formed the floor of their cage. Parker also revealed during his circus days a particular flair for publicity, one of his favourite stunts involving the display of advertisements on the side of an elephant that paraded along public thoroughfares, a technique he later employed at a disc-jockey convention in Nashville to draw attention to his client Eddy Arnold. The circus stunts, involving midgets, elephants and novelty giveaways, continued into the early years of managing Presley, but acquiring first-hand information about Parker has never been a simple task, as he seems to evoke a tight-lipped loyalty among his clients and professional contacts, many of whom have

been associated with him for lengthy periods, and even among his former clients. Eddy Arnold, for instance, still refuses to discuss his former manager, although in his autobiography, 'It's A Long Way From Chester County', he writes: 'When Tom's your manager, he's all you. He lives and breathes his artist'. As far as his military title goes, Parker did not achieve the rank of Colonel in the U.S. Army – the title is definitely honorary, and was bestowed on him by the Governor of the State of Tennessee in 1953. Not unnaturally, he was very proud of the honour, and has called himself 'Colonel' ever since – the epithet suited his huge ambition and determination to succeed with Elvis, and reflected the power that he was later to wield.

During the second half of 1955, Parker began to be personally involved with not only Elvis, but also his parents and with Bob Neal and Sam Phillips. He had ambitious plans that would involve major changes, although these could only be pursued after he had persuaded Neal to relinquish Presley's management and Phillips to sell the artist's recording contract to a much bigger record label with established national (and international) distribution. The first priority, of course, was to convince Elvis, Vernon and Gladys of his honourable intentions – while both

Elvis and his father seem to have taken to the Colonel immediately, Gladys proved to be rather more reluctant for Elvis to alter his business arrangements, as he was bound by several contracts, with Sun Records, with Bob Neal and also with the Louisiana Hayride. Parker sought help from Whitey Ford, a country performer whom Gladys admired, and Ford was able to convince her of the Colonel's honesty, and that his intention was to facilitate her son's success.

Parker's description of his agreement with Elvis was: 'It's a simple formula – I manage his business career, and I don't get involved with his private or social life'. History might have been significantly altered had the Colonel applied his undoubted business acumen to the more personal areas of Elvis's life. However, he took over management at a point where the singer's career was moving into top gear, following the release of his fifth (and last) single for Sun, *Mystery Train/I Forgot To Remember To Forget*, the former of which is the track many critics and fans regard as being the finest cut by Presley during his time with Sun Records. It was a song written and recorded (on Sun) by R&B singer Junior Parker, whose single was credited to Little Junior's Blue Flames when released a few years previously. The Presley version was released during August 1955, while *Baby Let's Play House* was still listed on the charts – *Mystery Train* became Elvis's biggest hit and biggest seller for Sun, and topped the country charts during the following November, coinciding with the important disc-jockey convention held in Nashville.

Sam Phillips received several offers for Elvis's contract, and gave Parker permission to negotiate the most advantageous deal – Columbia's Mitch Miller enquired about the asking price, but when told it was $20,000, retorted, 'No artist is worth that kind of money', and shortly afterwards, the comparatively new Atlantic label offered $25,000, but were told that it wasn't enough. Eventually, RCA signed Elvis – Parker was known to several executives of the company, as both Eddy Arnold and Hank Snow were also part of the company's roster, and the negotiations were conducted with A&R man Steve Sholes, while simultaneous deals were being worked out with Jean and Julian Aberbach, who ran Hill and Range Music Inc., the company which would publish all the songs Elvis would be recording. Parker's target was $50,000, but he eventually settled for $40,000, RCA contributing $25,000 and Hill and Range $15,000, of which Sam Phillips received $35,000 and Elvis himself $5,000, a sum in lieu of royalties outstanding from his Sun recordings. In late November 1955, RCA Records became (and remained until his death) Presley's record label, and reissued all five Sun singles, although allowing Sun to fulfil orders until the end of the year, after which Sam Phillips ceased to have rights to any of Elvis's recordings.

Meanwhile, the Colonel's assistant, Tom Diskin, was making plans for Elvis for 1956, including appearances on television, while RCA were also planning – their intention was to promote their new signing in the R&B and pop markets, as well as in the country music field, where he was already a fast rising star, the disc jockeys at the Nashville convention having voted him the most promising new male singer of 1955 (in retrospect, one of the most accurate judgements ever made).

Neither Sam Phillips nor Bob Neal have ever publicly admitted to regrets at losing Elvis – Neal was still working in radio and running his record shop, and seems to have been pleased that Parker took over, doubtless being aware that someone was needed who could devote themselves fully to Presley's career, and who would have a wider range of useful contacts. He later became Johnny Cash's manager, before moving to Nashville, where he was involved with the careers of several big country music stars. The $35,000 Phillips received seems laughable today, but at the time, it was an unprecedented amount for a record company to pay for a new artist, and Steve Sholes undoubtedly laid his job on the line when he offered the sum on RCA's behalf – for 1955, it was a brave gamble. Subsequently, Phillips has explained: 'You can't figure an artist's [commercial] life for more than six months' – he needed the money to promote other promising Sun artists like Carl Perkins, and could see no reason why he would be unable to find other young singers who would prove at least as successful as Elvis Presley.

FROM HEARTBREAK HOTEL TO UNCLE SAM

Right: Elvis onstage at a benefit concert in Tupelo with the Jordanaires and Scotty Moore, and (below) the most notorious pompadour of the 1950s in preparation.

Steve Sholes was RCA's Artistes and Repertoire Director for country & western and for R&B, and had acquired a reputation during his more than twenty years with the company for discovering and nurturing new talent. His past successes included two former clients of Colonel Tom Parker – country singers Eddy Arnold and Hank Snow – as well as the remarkable Chet Atkins. Atkins was signed to RCA during the 1940s initially as an artist, but later worked extensively as a session guitarist on recordings by others, and by 1956 had also become a part-time producer. For the first twelve years of Presley's contract with RCA Sholes and Atkins were jointly responsible for guiding his recording career in conjunction with Elvis himself. Elvis played a vital role in selecting material and polishing it in the studio with his musicians, while Colonel Parker, by establishing a tight control over the amount of material recorded by his charge, and how much of it was released by RCA, also played an important part.

Chet Atkins was particularly pleased when Sholes invited him to assemble a group of studio musicians to record with Elvis in RCA's Nashville studio during the first half of January, 1956: 'I'd been hearing about Elvis because he was so hot in Texas and Louisiana', Chet later recalled. 'I knew it was a very smart deal because all RCA had to do was spread that popularity, which they had the power to do because of their world-wide distributorship.' Atkins was quite correct – despite the fact that Sam Phillips had made great records with Elvis, he had been unable to sell them in large quantities across America. There was a very big difference between Sun Records, with one office and a minute staff, relying on a

variety of independent distributors around the U.S.A., and RCA, who not only ran offices in New York, Nashville and Los Angeles, but also possessed nation-wide distribution and had connections with international licensees who could reach a vast overseas audience.

Atkins was happy to continue with Scotty Moore and Bill Black, who had worked on the Sun tracks with Elvis but, unaware that Elvis now worked with D. J. Fontana, also hired a drummer for the sessions – the unfortunate studio player, whose identity remains unknown, was

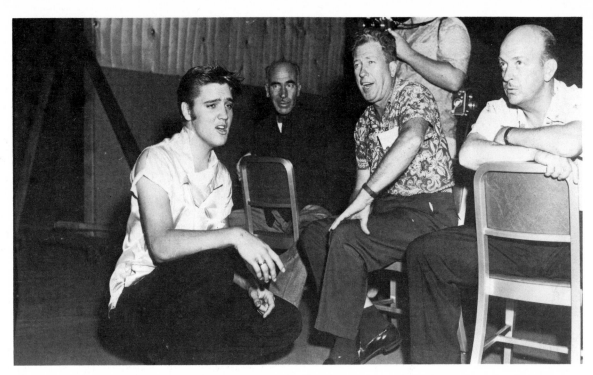

not used, and thus missed fame by a whisker. Other recruits were Nashville session pianist Floyd Cramer and three backing singers, Ben and Brock Speer from the Brock Family group and Gordon Stoker, first tenor with the country/gospel quartet, the Jordanaires, whom Elvis had admired on the Grand Ole Opry and who would subsequently sing on many Presley recordings. Chet also made himself available as an additional guitarist.

Today, RCA Records is situated in an impressive office and studio complex on Nashville's famed Music Row, and is known as the world's foremost country music label, but in 1956 their Tennessee operation was modest. Recording sessions took place at 1525 McGavock Street, which was owned by the Methodist Television, Radio and Film Commission, and where conditions were primitive and little better than those at Sam Phillips' studio in Memphis – if an echo effect was required, the musicians were forced to set up their equipment in a stairwell!

Elvis had spent the festive season with his family at their home at 1414 Getwell Road in Memphis, where they had lived since mid-1955, and a couple of days after his twenty-first birthday celebrations, he set off for Nashville along with Scotty, Bill, D.J., Colonel Parker and the latter's long-serving assistant, Tom Diskin. Scotty remembered feeling slight apprehension: 'I was afraid they'd try to clean

up our act, try to regiment us' – in fact, the RCA men weren't planning any radical changes, although Presley's new records would sound significantly different from the Sun releases. As Chet Atkins noted, 'We tried to do similar things to what Sam Phillips had done with tape echo and bass flapping, but of course there was a fear that maybe we wouldn't do the same thing. Maybe we'd put something in the record that people wouldn't accept, then they'd say that RCA had ruined him'.

Additionally, Steve Sholes was under heavy pressure from the RCA hierarchy in New York for a quick return on their extensive investment in Elvis. Sholes told David Dalton in 1968: 'A story was going round Nashville that I was the biggest fool that ever came down the 'pike, because we would never be able to make the kind of records he made with Sam Phillips. The truth is we didn't, because by the time we got around to making *Heartbreak Hotel*, his style had evolved a lot, and we were making a new sound that was very different even from the original sound that Elvis had put together'. This 'new sound' was based on the wild rockabilly of the Sun days, but it was fuller – due mainly to the extra voices and additional instrumentation – and smoother, with Scotty's guitar sounding less jagged, and Elvis's voice less frantic and better controlled. The 'new sound' was also extremely commercial.

The outstanding track of the five re-

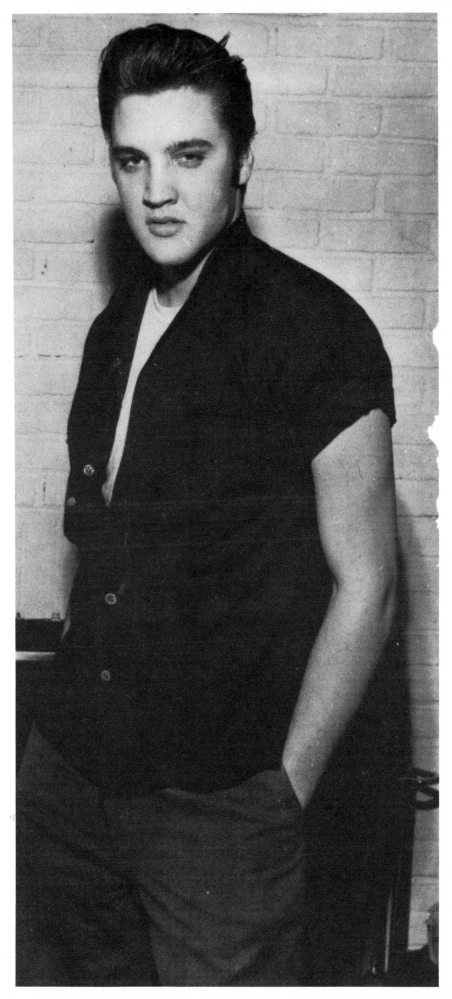

corded in early January was the ultra-dramatic *Heartbreak Hotel*, which became Presley's first bona fide smash hit, and remains one of the best-loved songs in popular music, appealing to a far wider range of listeners than any of the Sun tracks (although RCA's distribution meant that far more people were quickly aware of it), with Elvis's voice echoing supernaturally around the studio stairwell sending shivers down the spines of millions of record buyers. *Heartbreak Hotel* had been written specifically for Elvis by the little-known songwriting team of Mae Boren Axton (mother of country singer Hoyt Axton) and Tommy Durden. Mae lived in Jacksonville, Florida, where she combined work as schoolteacher and songwriter with publicity work on behalf of Colonel Tom Parker, whenever any of his acts came to town, and it was in this latter capacity that she had met and befriended Elvis even before he was officially connected with Parker. As well as recording one of the first radio interviews with Elvis, she had advised him to 'go with Colonel Tom Parker', and promised the youngster, perhaps more in hope than expectation, that she would write him his first million-selling hit.

One night, her partner, Tommy Durden, arrived at the Axton house with a newspaper story about a man who had committed suicide and left a note that read 'I walk a lonely street'. Some years later, Mae recalled 'That really upset me, and I said to Tommy "Everyone in the world, whether they're rich or poor, has someone who cares. When this man's somebody sees this story, they'll be heartbroken, because there's a heartbreak hotel at the end of every lonely street". Tommy just said "Let's write it", so we did.' Another of Mae's songwriting partners, Glen Reeves, was also present, but left saying he wanted nothing to do with 'such a silly song', but when it was completed, Mae felt sure that it would be perfect for Elvis, and wanted to provide him with a demonstration record sounding just like him. The demo made by Tommy sounded too sweet, so she prevailed upon Glen Reeves to cut another demo, offering him as compensation one third of the music publishing rights. Although Reeves did as he was asked, he still insisted that he wanted nothing else to do with the song, and thereby turned down a share in a multi-million selling hit.

Mae Axton gave the demo to Elvis at the 1955 disc-jockey convention in Nashville, and he was very impressed – according to Tommy Durden, the completed record was remarkably similar to Reeves's demo, and he later noted 'I was convinced when I

Right: The casual look, and opposite, moody and magnificent.

heard the record that Elvis was even breathing in the same places as Glen did on the dub' – and the idea of songwriters producing demo discs performed in a style very similar to the way in which it was envisaged Elvis might sing them subsequently became common practice. Other precedents for Elvis's career were also set by the first RCA session in Nashville – where most artists rehearsed their material prior to a recording session, Elvis arrived with nothing prepared. He would listen to a batch of demos, quickly select those he liked, then work out arrangements on the spot with his musicians. 'I work with ear musicians, not sheet musicians', he told a reporter. 'They're great – you just hum or whistle, sing a tune for them once, then they get to work, and inside a minute or two, the joint's jumping.'

Scotty Moore confirms Elvis's role as instigator: 'If you had to give anyone credit for producing those records, it was probably Elvis himself, because it was up to him to weed through the pile of material and demos that were brought in. Once he found one he wanted to try, it was just a group effort to work it out – everyone made suggestions, and sometimes songs would be thrown out after we'd run through them a couple of times.'

That first historic session on January 10 and 11 yielded five completed songs, of which *Heartbreak Hotel* and *I Was The One* were chosen as the two sides of the second RCA single by Elvis (the first having been a reissue of *Mystery Train/I Forgot To Remember To Forget*), which was released in late January 1956, while *I'm Counting On You, Money Honey* (a 1953 R&B hit originally cut by the Drifters, then led by Clyde McPhatter) and *I Got A Woman* (actually the first RCA Presley track completed, and another R&B hit, from 1954, by its composer, Ray Charles) were to appear on the singer's debut LP, *Elvis Presley*, released the following April. Jordanaire Gordon Stoker told Jerry Hopkins: 'After the session, Elvis said that if any of the songs went big, he wanted us to record all his stuff with him, but we didn't think they'd go big, and in fact, we didn't think much about it at all. We didn't even remember his name really'. Chet Atkins had much more confidence: 'I knew he would be a

Right: Elvis entertains his early fans, 1956, and (below) a typically flamboyant onstage pose from the same year.

smash because he was so hot, and when a guy gets that hot, everything he makes is going to be a hit.'

After the session was completed, Elvis and his band returned to the road for more concert dates which had been booked by Bob Neal who, on paper at least, was still manager until March 15, 1956. Meanwhile, Parker was master-minding rather more important deals – on January 28, the day after a thirty-five dollar booking in Texas, Elvis, Scotty, Bill and D.J. flew to New York for the first of six networked T.V. appearances, each of which would earn the singer $1200.

The 30-minute Saturday night variety programme 'Jackie Gleason's Stage Show' was hosted by Tommy and Jimmy Dorsey, two brothers who had led celebrated Big Bands, but was screened at the same time as the popular 'Perry Como Show', whose ratings were substantially superior. Elvis had been booked as one of several desperate measures undertaken in an attempt to boost audience figures, after the show's executive producer, Jack Philbin, had seen a photograph of the singer which moved him to remark, 'This kid is the guitar-playing Marlon Brando'. Brando, like James Dean, was the epitome of the rebellious anti-hero for many American teenagers, and his films had become box-office successes. Philbin hoped that Elvis could have a similar effect on the ratings of 'Stage Show'.

The first show featuring Elvis saw him wearing a light-coloured oversized sports jacket, sneering at the camera, shaking his legs and swivelling his hips as he sang *Blue Suede Shoes* and *Heartbreak Hotel*. His

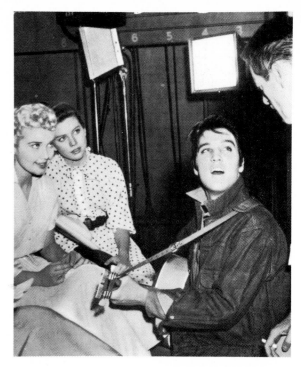

performance was a revelation, since nothing similar had ever been seen before on network television, and the show attracted an avalanche of mail, split between those wanting to know more about this 'extraordinary new singer' – Elvis was still little known outside the American South – and those critical of what were called 'his lewd movements'. He made five further appearances on Stage Show, but ratings remained poor, and the show was soon dropped. Elvis himself reaped considerable benefit from it, however – *Heartbreak Hotel* shot to the top of the 'Billboard' Hot 100 on March 24, and noted film producer Hal Wallis contacted Tom Parker and arranged a screen test for Elvis. He was also featured by both Steve Allen and Milton Berle on their prestigious T.V. variety shows. This interest pushed up his value as a live attraction, and once the dates organized by Bob Neal were out of the way, Colonel Parker was able to ask, and get, $10,000 or more for the 'Elvis Presley Show'.

Within a few weeks, Elvis became a favourite with teenage record buyers and radio listeners all over the United States, although he was one of the last to discover his new-found fame due to a punishing work schedule. In the days after the first T.V. show, he was recording at RCA's New York studio, then rushed away for two days of live concerts before returning to Manhattan for further recording plus another T.V. show. What made this

workload even more exhausting was that previously contracted live dates in the South and vitally important T.V. shows in New York meant round trips of several thousand miles. After the final 'Stage Show' for instance, Elvis was driven from New York to Los Angeles to perform at the Coliseum, then on to San Diego, also in Southern California, for another T.V. show, followed by another drive to a concert in Denver, Colorado. During March, and not suprisingly in the circumstances, Elvis collapsed from exhaustion in Jacksonville, Florida, and was taken to hospital where a doctor prescribed complete rest for a week. However, the following morning saw Elvis, suitably refreshed and with bags packed, carrying on with the tour.

On April 1 Elvis was in Hollywood for his screen test, playing a scene opposite veteran actor Frank Faylen, who had been persuaded to take part during a break from filming 'Gunfight At The O.K. Corral'. Passing the test without any problem, Elvis was signed to a seven-year, three-film, contract with Paramount, for which he would receive an initial $100,000 for the first film, $150,000 for the second and $200,000 for the third. 1956 was

proving to be a phenomenal year for Elvis, with his popularity building at a rate that was quite unprecedented in popular music. There was only one low point, which occurred in the latter half of April in the neon-lit resort city of Las Vegas, Nevada. Colonel Parker had booked Elvis for a two-week engagement at the Frontier Hotel. As most of the visitors to Las Vegas were middle-aged, their interest in the 'King Of Rock'n'Roll', as music magazines had begun to call Elvis, was limited to curiosity, with the result that the audience response for the Frontier shows was cool to the point where Parker cancelled the second week. Of course, everywhere else Elvis appeared was packed with frenzied screaming fans.

In early May Elvis was back in Memphis, and played several concerts as part of the local Cotton Picking Jamboree, after which he took a few days off to help his parents with their move into a new house, which he told a journalist he had bought for his mother: 'It's something she always wanted but never talked about – it was as if she didn't want anyone to know about her dreams, but I knew, and I wanted to get my mother a home'. 1034 Audubon Drive cost Elvis $40,000, and he

Elvis and his parents outside their new home at 1034 Audubon Drive, Memphis.

Above: The kind of publicity shot which broke female hearts, (right) with the fans outside the Audubon Drive house and (bottom) showing off his new car.

also arranged for the building of a swimming pool and a high wall, the latter to keep out his more adventurous fans. Despite spikes in the top of the wall, the most intrepid fans still found ways to enter the grounds – once inside, they stared through windows, rang the doorbell, and even stole washing from the line! The neighbours complained, a few clubbing together in an attempt to buy the house, but Elvis's response was to offer to buy their homes instead.

After the 'Stage Show' appearances, which were judged a success, Elvis was booked to appear with comedian Milton Berle on NBC-T.V. for shows in April and June. Berle was a very popular T.V. personality, nicknamed 'the thief of bad gags' and, unlike the Dorsey Brothers, had a huge audience. The first show caused quite a stir, but the second, watched by over forty million viewers, marked a turning point in Presley's career, when the controversy over his supposedly vulgar stage movements suddenly became a national topic for discussion. Leading American religious crusader Billy Graham said, 'I wouldn't let my daughter walk across the street to see Elvis Presley perform', while Ed Sullivan, who hosted the highest-rated variety shows on American T.V., proclaimed, 'I wouldn't have Elvis Presley on my show at any time'. More stinging remarks came from critics in newspapers, including Jack Gould of the 'New York Times', who observed 'Mr. Presley has no discernible singing ability. His speciality is rhythm songs, which he renders in an undistinguished whine; his phrasing, if it can be called that, consists of stereotyped variations that go with a beginner's aria in a bath tub. For the ear, he is an unutterable bore'. Jack O'Brien, writing in the New York 'Journal-American', decreed: 'He can't sing a lick and makes up for vocal shortcomings with the weirdest and plainly planned suggestive animation short of an Aborigine's mating dance'.

Several newspapers suggested that Presley was some kind of threat to society and would inflict permanent damage on teenagers, and stories began to appear about teenage mob violence perpetrated by those who had been listening to rock'n'roll records. A Mayor in New Jersey banned all rock concerts, there

were bonfires of rock'n'roll discs, and operators of juke boxes refused to have certain records on their machines. One angry New York minister even called Elvis 'a whirling dervish of sex'.

Elvis was surprised and somewhat hurt by the criticism, and said: 'I've tried to figure it out, and I don't see how they think someone just singing and dancing would contribute to juvenile delinquency. I wouldn't do anything vulgar in front of anyone, especially children, because my folks didn't bring me up that way. I don't do anything bad when I work, I just move with the music, it's the way I feel. Some people tap their feet, some just snap their fingers, and I just started doing them all together'. Even Gladys Presley was persuaded to make a rare public statement, in which she said, 'My boy wouldn't do anything bad. He's a good boy, a boy who has never forgotten his church upbringing, and he hasn't changed a bit'.

What annoyed Elvis most was a nick-name he'd been given by a journalist – Elvis the Pelvis – which many writers had subsequently picked up. 'I don't like being called Elvis the Pelvis', he said in a 1956 interview that appeared on a cardboard record given away with the magazine 'T.V. Guide', which is now one of the rarest of all Elvis Presley records. 'I mean, it's one of the most childish expressions I ever heard! But if they want to call me that, there ain't nothing I can do about it, so I have to accept it, like I accept the good with the bad, and the bad with the good.'

Press criticism was just one of the many pressures building up on Elvis – since the second Milton Berle T.V. show, life, to quote D.J. Fontana, had become 'like a battlefield' – Elvis had to be constantly protected from over-enthusiastic fans, and on tour he was a virtual prisoner. 'It's impossible now to leave my hotel room', he told a scribe, 'I remember one night I woke up starving, but I didn't dare go out

PRIVATE US53310761

Speculation concerning Elvis joining the U. S. Army had been rife, and Colonel Tom Parker had paid close attention to the sentiments expressed both by fans, who claimed to be heartbroken and angry at the prospect of losing their idol for two years at the height of his popularity, and the more cynical critics, who were sure that great care had been taken to make certain that the celebrated recruit would be given an 'easy ride'.

Parker's ambitions for his client (or 'my boy', the name by which he invariably referred to Elvis in public), extended well beyond the teenage rock'n'roll audience to embrace a career dominated by films and records aimed at punters of all age groups. He realized that despite the highly signifi-

cant broadening of Elvis's appeal in terms of his musical repertoire (epitomized by the EP of gospel songs and the Christmas album), most adult Americans continued to be antagonized by the strongly delineated image of rebellious youth, complete with strange clothes and especially his uncouth stage mannerisms. Parker's reasoning led to the conclusion that if Elvis were to join the Army as an ordinary soldier, who was allowed no special privileges, public opinion of him would mellow, while there seemed no reason to suppose, in view of his incredible popularity, that teenage fans would shift their allegiance elsewhere during Presley's enforced absence from the spotlight.

Elvis, who by now had come to trust the Colonel's judgement implicitly, agreed to this course of action, telling a reporter in Memphis: 'I reckon I'll be able to handle the Army assignment O.K. I've been working since I was about fourteen – had to. I've worked in factories, drove a truck, cut grass for a living, and did a hitch in a defence plant. I'll do whatever they tell me, and I won't be asking for any special favours'. When the journalist enquired whether Elvis expected to return to music after the two year hiatus, the singer replied, 'I hope my fans will welcome me back – maybe I'll start a new career as a ballad singer or a singer of spirituals'.

When the call-up notice arrived, it was hardly a surprise in view of the earlier medical check, although it arrived considerably sooner than had been expected. Paramount Pictures in particular found the military's timing not only surprising, but also inconvenient, as they had invested $300,000 preparing for the next Elvis film, 'King Creole', and suspected that the sum would be wasted and lost

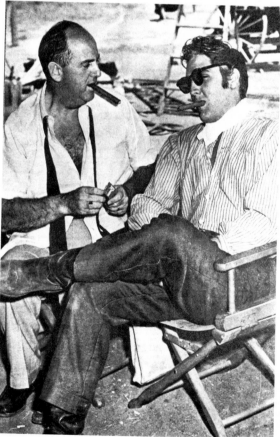

A rare shot of Elvis with a cigar – the Colonel's cheroot wasn't quite such a novelty!

Opposite: A portrait taken in 1958.

64

Right: A moment to tickle the ivories on a film set in 1958.

Below right: Elvis with his co-stars in 'King Creole'; (left) Carolyn Jones and (right) Dolores Hart.

completely if their star were to join the Army, as he had been instructed, in January 1958. Accordingly, Paramount wrote to Milton Bowers, the chairman of the Memphis draft board, requesting a postponement, but were informed that only Elvis himself could ask for deferment. Elvis then addressed a personal letter to the board in which he stressed that while he wasn't asking for a delay for his own sake, the film people who had been so helpful in launching and improving his career now stood to lose a considerable sum of money. As a result, the request was granted, and the call up deferred until late March.

Milton Bowers, who had been inundated with hate mail and telephone calls from irate Elvis fans ever since the draft notice had been delivered, now found himself on the receiving end of equally unpleasant letters and calls from Presley's critics, furious and supposedly indignant that a 'mere rock'n'roll singer' should be granted such special favours by the U. S. Army – Bowers was interviewed almost daily by the newspapers until he reached the point where he began to wish he had never heard the name Elvis Presley, exclaiming, 'I'm fed up to the teeth! I eat, sleep and drink Elvis Presley . . .', tempering his bitterness slightly by adding, 'With all due respect to Elvis, who's a nice boy, we've drafted people who are far, far more important than he is', but

undoing any vaguely charitable nuances by adding, perhaps rather callously, 'After all, when you take him out of the entertainment business, what have you got left? A truck driver'.

In early January, Elvis took the train from Memphis to Los Angeles to begin shooting 'King Creole' in Hollywood, with an accompanying entourage of friends and business associates. At every station along the way, small armies of fans waited, many convinced that this would be their last chance to see Elvis in the flesh – for Colonel Parker, this was all welcome grist to the publicity mill, and supported

his conviction that not only would his client's career survive, it would positively prosper from the impending two-year lay off.

'King Creole' was loosely based on a Harold Robbins novel, 'A Stone For Danny Fisher', and was directed by Michael Curtiz, a Hungarian who had scored notable successes during the 1930s and 1940s with films like 'Mildred Pierce' and the immortal 'Casablanca'. While 'King Creole' could not be expected to match the majesty of the latter classic, it proved to be one of Curtiz's best post-war films, his work overall during this period

having achieved somewhat less critical acclaim.

Elvis played the role of Danny Fisher, a bus boy (waiter) at the Blue Quarter nightclub in the celebrated French Quarter of New Orleans, who becomes a singer at the King Creole club. The plot provides him with associations with a prostitute (played by Carolyn Jones), a gang of crooks (led by Walter Matthau) and a pretty girl named Nellie (marking a reunion with Dolores Hart, who had previously appeared in 'Loving You'), and after much action and several good songs, Jones and Matthau meet appropriately final ends, and Elvis and Dolores Hart live happily ever after.

Elvis subsequently cited 'King Creole' as his favourite film, a view with which many critics have agreed — among the favourable reviews received by the film came rare praise from the 'New York Times', whose critic called it 'A surprisingly colourful and lively drama, with Elvis Presley doing some surprisingly credible acting flanked by a dandy supporting cast'. Among a number of good songs on the soundtrack were the title track and *Trouble* (two of the three Leiber/Stoller songs in the movie) and *Hard Headed Woman*, while another song, *Crawfish* is notable as the first occasion on which Elvis was joined on record by another solo singer, Kitty White, who

contributed the one word 'Crawfish' to the song.

Part of the film was shot on location in New Orleans, which inevitably caused problems with crowd control for both the film crew and the police, a situation that was hardly improved by the nomination of an 'Elvis Presley Day' locally, when local authorities gave the city's schoolchildren an official day's holiday, doubtless in the knowledge that if such a day off had not been declared officially, the pupils would have taken one unofficially.

With filming completed, Elvis returned to Memphis to bid a tearful farewell to his beloved parents. His mother was particularly upset that her only son was joining the Army – she still had nightmares about what might happen to him. These terrified her so much that she had confided in friends that she wished Elvis would abandon his singing career, and instead acquire a business and settle down with a wife – although one person to whom she had not revealed her fears was Elvis himself.

At 6.30 a.m. on Monday, March 24, 1958, after an all-night party with his family and friends, Elvis arrived at the Memphis Draft Board to enlist in the U.S. Army. Despite the early hour and the bad weather – it was cold and wet – there were several fans waiting, while Colonel Parker was also there, of course, handing out free balloons advertising the forthcoming 'King Creole' movie – he had planned to maximize the publicity surrounding Elvis's enlistment, and had assembled a large corps of newspaper men to record the transformation of Elvis from rock'n'roll star to soldier. The Army, welcoming any publicity that might encourage further recruits, even allowed Parker and a team of press men to accompany Elvis, with a view to documenting his first few days in the service of his country.

Accompanied by several other new recruits from the Memphis area, Elvis went to the Kennedy Veterans Hospital for medical tests, after which he was sworn in, given his U. S. Army private's number – US53310761 – and informed that his monthly pay would amount to $83.20, a dramatic drop from the $1,000 per week guaranteed him by RCA Records. During the late afternoon the new soldiers were driven towards Fort

Chaffee, Arkansas, stopping off at the Coffee Cup restaurant where the men were due to have a meal, but scores of Elvis fans, who had been following the bus in private cars, arrived and caused such a commotion that the soldiers were ordered back on the bus before they had finished their food and the bus sped away. Back at the Coffee Cup, souvenir-hunting fans and waitresses came close to blows over who should become the proud possessor of the place mat, cutlery and chair used by Elvis, and there were several hundred more fans waiting at Fort Chaffee when the tired and hungry soldiers finally arrived there in the evening.

Next morning they were up at 5.30 a.m., to find the Colonel and the photographers waiting to take pictures of Elvis tucking into the egg, sausage, toast and coffee provided by Uncle Sam, a prelude to another exhausting day which would include several hours of aptitude tests, whose results would supposedly indicate to which military task each recruit was best suited. After lunch came the traditional Army haircuts, the event which most of the press men were eagerly anticipating, when Elvis's trademark sideburns and hairstyle would be re-

moved. Like all his colleagues, Elvis was given the standard Army crewcut by the barber, James Peterson, who tossed the legendary sideburns into the air with a flourish. 'Hair today, gone tomorrow' punned Elvis, while Colonel Parker made great play of the fact that the hair was worth a fortune, but then ensured that it was swept up and destroyed with all the other pompadours – in the confusion, Elvis neglected to pay Peterson his fee of sixty-five cents.

Elvis's second day at Fort Chaffee saw him issued with his uniform – Parker tried to slip a string tie in with Presley's kit, but the latter pushed it back at his manager, and observers noted that it seemed as if Elvis was beginning to get annoyed at Parker's somewhat heavy-handed efforts to wring the maximum publicity from what should, perhaps, have been a rather more dignified event. That afternoon, at a press conference, it was announced that Elvis would be stationed at Fort Hood, Texas, for basic combat training with the 2nd Armoured Division. Elvis confidently told the reporters: 'You name it – I've been all over Texas. I got my start in music around Houston' (probably a reference to his live shows in the Houston

Above: Elvis after his medical check at the Memphis Draft Board, 1957.

Right: Elvis with a fan, Gloria Mowels, during his training period in Texas, 1958.

Opposite: Private US53310761 Elvis Presley.

area in 1954). When asked how he was being treated by his fellow soldiers, he reported: 'They've been swell – they treat me like everyone else, and they consider themselves for what they are. Just G.I.s, the same as me. That's how I see it'. After this, a General announced: 'I feel the Army has shown that it is trying to make an ordinary soldier out of Mr. Presley, the same as the other fine young men who are with us, and that he's been afforded no special privileges. I believe Presley should make a tremendous success of his Army operation – he has conducted himself in a marvellous manner'.

American newspaper readers lapped up the news of Elvis in the Army with considerable interest, as every minute detail about what he was doing, eating and saying was reported, but when he arrived at Ford Hood on the following Friday, an Army information officer called a halt to all the publicity. 'He has a mission, and we have a mission,' she said, 'and we expect to perform them mutually. Hereafter, there will be no more interviews or pictures taken during his training', whereupon the reporters and Colonel Parker (the latter no doubt mindful of his supposedly 'military' title) obediently departed, but if the information officer had supposed that things would now revert to normal, she would soon discover how wrong were her assumptions, as Fort Hood began to receive thousands of letters and telephone calls from Elvis fans, throwing the communications system into total chaos, while every weekend saw the camp besieged by hundreds of fans peering through the wire fences in the hope of catching a glimpse of Elvis.

Despite the week-long series of stories in the newspapers showing Elvis being a normal soldier, many still believed that he would receive special treatment that would enable him to continue to perform, not only to civilian audiences, but also within the Army – Colonel Parker received several requests from high-ranking officers begging for Elvis to appear at military charity shows, but his reply was simple and direct – that there would be no public performance from Elvis Presley during his time in the service.

While he was stationed at Fort Hood, Elvis became friends with a local disc jockey, Eddie Fadal from Waco, Texas, and spent many off-duty hours at Fadal's house, while Anita Wood, a Memphis T.V. personality, disc jockey and singer, who had met Elvis at the beginning of 1958, and had become his most recent girlfriend, was a frequent weekend visitor. The tough training schedule lasted for two months, after which the recruits were allowed a two-week leave, which Elvis took in Memphis, looking very fit, and apparently having lost weight. He took the opportunity to attend the local première of 'King Creole', and made two trips to Nashville to record for RCA, which would be the only recording sessions he would undertake during his stint in the Army.

70

RCA were desperate for new material, as there was nothing 'in the can' but the 'King Creole' soundtrack plus a couple of unreleased tracks recorded the previous year. The company obviously wanted to stockpile sufficient Presley recordings to tide them over until his national service was completed, but the Colonel had other ideas. Having virtually flooded the market in 1956/7, Parker decided that the best way to sustain interest in Elvis during the period of enforced inactivity was to release a very few records, and thus leave the fans wanting more.

It was a plan which worked perfectly – only three new singles were released in 1958, and just two in 1959 (aside from *Don't/I Beg Of You*, which was released before the Army stint in January 1958, and predated the Parker strategy). The other three 1958 singles, *Wear My Ring Around Your Neck*, *Hard Headed Woman* (from 'King Creole') and the double-A side, *I Got Stung/One Night*, were all massive hits, as were the 1959 releases, another double-A sided single in *A Fool Such As I/I Need Your Love Tonight* and *A Big Hunk O'Love*. The last two of these five single releases (plus *I Got Stung*) were recorded in Nashville during the two weeks leave, overseen by Chet Atkins, and featured musicians who subsequently became notable practitioners of the 'Nashville Sound' – Hank Garland, who shared guitar duties with Atkins, Floyd Cramer on piano, Bob Moore playing bass, and the Jordanaires supplying backing vocals were all top-notch session musicians who refined the sound and image of country music from its twangy hillbilly hayseed roots to a smoother, more sophisticated urban style. D.J. Fontana also took part in the sessions, but for the first time (commencing with the 1958 sessions in Nashville), Scotty Moore and Bill Black were conspicuous by their absence. Both were now based full time in Memphis – Scotty worked with artists on the Fernwood record label, although he would later move to Nashville, and be involved in future Presley sessions, but Bill Black would never again play with Presley. Black formed his own band, the Bill Black Combo, who scored over a dozen hits on the Memphis-based Hi label between 1959 and 1964, including *White Silver Sands, Blue Tango* and a memorable instrumental version of the song which he had recorded with Elvis, *Don't Be Cruel*, before his premature death in October, 1965.

Despite his recording commitments, much of Elvis's two weeks away from the Army was spent with this parents and/or Anita Wood, to whom he gave a diamond ring, leading to several newspapers suggesting that the couple had become engaged. Anita fuelled rumours by recording *I'll Wait Forever* for Sun. Absence having apparently indeed made the heart grow fonder (at least where his parents were concerned), Elvis arranged for Vernon and Gladys to live close to the Fort Hood base in a mobile home at the end of his leave, but this proved unsatisfactory, and they moved to a three-bedroomed house, where Elvis was also allowed to live 'off-base'.

While this was evidently not precisely standard Army procedure, it was probably regarded as desirable in the special circumstances, added to which it enabled Elvis to be close to his mother, about whom he was becoming increasingly worried. Gladys Presley had suffered from ill health for some years, but was now particularly unwell, having difficulty in walking and seeming constantly tired.

When his wife took a turn for the worse, Vernon Presley decided that she should return to Memphis in order to be near the family doctor. Within a short time, she was admitted to a private ward at the new Methodist Hospital, where doctors diagnosed hepatitis, a liver complaint. However, she continued to deteriorate, becoming seriously ill to the point where Elvis was granted emergency leave to visit her. During the early hours of Thursday, August 14, she suffered a fatal heart attack, and Elvis, who was asleep at Graceland, was woken and given the sad news, to which he responded with a mixture of shock and disbelief. The person whom he loved most in the world was gone – the very strong emotional attachment between mother and son had continued from birth to his days of stardom, and he had frequently contacted her by telephone when he was away from home, as he still depended on her utterly for many things. 'I was the only child, and Mama was always right with me', he said.

Elvis and Vernon would not allow an

autopsy to be performed on Gladys, and because of this, no one can be certain of the reason for her death, although it seems most likely that it was connected with her weight problem. A close family friend, quoted in Jerry Hopkins' biography, 'Elvis', explained: 'She wanted to look good for Elvis, to be thin and attractive, but she stayed heavy and began to put on weight, so she began to take diet pills, and I guess they became a habit with her, and then she switched to alcohol. It was sad . . . All she wanted was to make Elvis proud and, of course, he was proud, but she kept on taking those pills and drinking, and finally her big ol' heart gave out'. 400 guests were invited to the funeral service, and Gladys's favourite gospel group, the Blackwoods, were flown specially from North Carolina. Three thousand Elvis fans stood outside the funeral home in Memphis, silently paying their respects, and Gladys was buried at the Forest Lawn Cemetery. Elvis paid for a ten-foot high marble monument – a statue of Christ with two angels kneeling at either side – with an inscription that read: 'Gladys Smith Presley April 25, 1912 – Aug. 14, 1958. Beloved wife of Vernon Presley and mother of Elvis Presley. She was the sunshine of our home'. Elvis was overcome with grief, and a reporter at the graveside heard him saying: 'Oh God, everything I have is gone'.

Elvis's mother, Gladys Presley, shortly before her premature death.

The Army gave Elvis an extra week's leave, and when he returned to Fort Hood, the second stage of his training was almost over, and it was announced that his unit would be stationed in West Germany. With 1300 other soldiers, Elvis left the United States on September 19 from the Army Marine Terminal in Brooklyn, New York, aboard the U.S.S. *General Randall*, an Army troop ship which took its name from that of a famous Confederate Army officer (incidentally, in the 'Love Me Tender' movie, Elvis's 'brother', Vance Reno, had supposedly served with Randall, although the choice of a ship with the same name was nothing more than coincidence).

Steve Sholes recorded the press conference given by Elvis just prior to his departure, and released it in March 1959, on RCA as an EP titled *Elvis Sails*. Elvis told the assembled newsmen: 'Before I was drafted, I'd been trying to arrange a European tour, but now I'll get to Europe anyway. I'm looking forward to my first furlough in Paris – I'd like to meet Brigitte Bardot!' When asked if the other soldiers gave him a rough time, he replied 'No sir. I was very surprised, and I've never met a nicer group of boys in my life. They

probably would have [given me a hard time] if it had been like everybody thought, that I wouldn't work, and I'd be given special treatment'. What would he do if rock'n'roll died while he was away? 'I'd probably starve to death', joked Elvis, 'but if it did happen, and I don't think it will, I'd make a serious try to get to the top in the movies – that would be my best chance'. Some reporters asked if he was taking his family with him to West Germany, to which came the answer, 'My father and grandmother are following in a few weeks, and they'll be living in a home near the post where I'll be stationed. I guess we'll get one of those small German cars – I still have three Cadillacs and a Lincoln, but they stay at home'. Then, as an Army band played versions of *Hound Dog* and *All Shook Up*, Elvis stepped aboard the ship – six times, for the benefit of all the cameramen. His cabin companion for the voyage was a diminutive country music guitarist named Charlie Hodge, who became a very close friend to Elvis, with whom he later worked for many years, looking after the star's instruments.

The *General Randall* arrived at Bremerhaven on October 1, where hundreds of German fans were waiting for a first glimpse of Elvis, although most were disappointed, as the soldiers were whisked aboard a train and taken to the Army station at Friedburg, a few miles north of Frankfurt, where Elvis was based for his seventeen months in Germany.

For the first three days, the local press were given access to Elvis, and the almost inevitable press conference was held, where the equally inevitable questions about girlfriends were asked, along with the familiar enquiries about the death of rock'n'roll and how he was being treated by his fellow soldiers. It was also announced that Elvis would be driving a scout jeep – a spokesman, whose comments seemed to reveal that the Army was still sensitive to suggestions that Elvis would be unable to cope with life as an ordinary infantryman, explained: 'The assignment of scout jeep driver is given to soldiers of above normal capacity – the soldier must be able to work on his own, map read and draw sketches, know tactics, and recognize the enemy and enemy weapons'.

There was another reason for this assignment that wasn't explained at the press conference – while training at Fort Hood, Elvis had perforated an eardrum on

Opposite top: Crowds surround the troop train bringing Elvis to the New York docks on his way to Germany.

Opposite bottom: Private Presley stealing a last look at his New York fan following before embarking for Europe.

Above: Arriving in Germany.

the shooting range, and was therefore given a job away from heavy gunfire, to prevent it happening again. His ears were, of course, precious to Elvis, and one of Gladys Presley's greatest worries had been for his hearing, as he had suffered from chronic earache as a child. Friends recall her saying to Elvis: 'You be careful of your ears – you know you play by ear and can't read music, so you should be careful'.

Vernon and Minnie Mae Presley, along with Memphis friends Red West and Lamar Fike, arrived in West Germany a few weeks after Elvis – his friends became increasingly important to him following his mother's death, and were frequently with him during off-duty hours. Initially, the party stayed at the Gruenwald Hotel in Bad Homburg, where most of the hotel guests were elderly, and therefore soon became distressed by the games Elvis

played with Lamar and Red after Army duties were finished for the day. In his book, 'Elvis: What Happened?', Red West recalled: 'We never stopped playing games – each week, we had a different kind of fight. We always had water pistols . . . then there were shaving cream fights, and all the time pushing and wrestling each other to the floor'. Their youthful high jinks finally led to the hotel management asking the party to leave, whereupon Elvis rented a house at Goethestrasse 14, Bad Nauheim, where the rent amounted to $800 per month, which was about four times the rate a German family would have expected to pay, but whose owners realized that Elvis had plenty of money.

As well as hiring a cook, Elvis also employed a secretary, Elizabeth Stefaniak, who dealt with the mountains of mail from German fans, although several young local inhabitants also discovered where Elvis lived and began to call at the house – Red West later noted: 'Generally speaking, the German fans seemed better mannered than the Americans – I mean, you could joke around with them, talk to them without getting ripped apart!' Nevertheless, the constant ringing on the doorbell became a nuisance to the point where Elvis arranged for a sign to be placed outside, on which was written in German, 'Autographs between 7.30 and 8.00 p.m. only, please'. Sometimes he would go out in person, still dressed in his Army fatigues, but more often, Red and Lamar collected the books and pieces of paper before retreating inside to forge Elvis's signature, something at which they became very skilful, as did Vernon and Minnie Mae.

Days for Elvis were long and tiring – after rising around 5.00 a.m., he would drive to the base in his white BMW sports car, before spending the rest of the daytime in his jeep with platoon leader Sergeant Ira Jones. Most evenings were spent relaxing at home, enjoying favourite snacks like fried potato sandwiches, or a mixture of peanut butter and mashed bananas on toast. This unusual diet, which was obviously high in fat content, would cause Elvis serious weight problems in the future, but since he was taking so much exercise as part of his Army duties, it had little effect on him at the time.

Elvis meets the stars of an ice show in Frankfurt, 1959.

Far left: Elvis meeting fans outside his rented house in Bad Nauheim, West Germany, during the summer of 1959, and (left) an evening autograph session at Bad Nauheim.

Below: A German press photograph of Elvis taken as he went on Army manoeuvres.

Right: With a sack of fan mail.

Below: An official U.S. Army photograph of Sergeant Elvis.

He generally tended to treat his Army service as a duty, a job that had to be done, and never complained about it in public, although Red West apparently remembered occasional bad moods, when Elvis would curse the situation in which he found himself. On one occasion, he said to Red, 'Man, what the hell am I doing here? That old Colonel, he could have fixed it'. Meanwhile, Red and Lamar sometimes complained to each other because they were paid so little by their boss – 'We got our three square meals a day, so I guess we couldn't complain – we were there because we wanted to be there, and nobody forced us, but the most we got was a few marks here and there'.

Newsmen were given little access to Presley during this period, and most of the stories that were published came via the 'Stars And Stripes', a newspaper designed for the Armed Services, although one enterprising German photographer inspired a story about Elvis having a German girlfriend, by persuading him to pose with a teenage girl named Margrit Buergin, whom Elvis liked and began to date, and whom he called his 'little puppy'. She began to receive hate mail from German fans, and the resulting newspaper stories certainly assisted in cooling the previously strong relationship with Anita Wood, the girl Elvis had left behind in Memphis.

Among the stories reported in 'Stars And Stripes' was one about a car accident involving Vernon Presley and Elizabeth Stefaniak – the car in which they were travelling turned over several times after crashing on the Frankfurt-Kassel autobahn, but miraculously, both escaped with minor injuries. Another newspaper report, in June 1959, concerned Elvis suffering an attack of tonsilitis, for which he was being hospitalized for a second time.

By far the most significant event that concerned Elvis, however, was not reported in the papers, this being his courtship of Priscilla Beaulieu, who was fifteen years old at the time, and would become his wife in 1967. She was the stepdaughter of an Air Force major stationed at Wiesbaden, and was introduced to Elvis by U.S. airman James Curry in 1959, when the girl was only fourteen. Elvis was very taken with the well-mannered, sophisticated young girl with the long

brown curly hair and the pretty face, and the two saw each other frequently, although they lived miles apart, which necessitated Lamar Fike making many long journeys in the car to collect her in the early evening, and to take her home later. Presley met many girls in Germany, but only Priscilla was to have a long lasting and profound effect on him, perhaps because, unlike the others, she seemed totally unaffected by his star status and behaved perfectly normally.

During the previous year, Vernon Presley had met his future second wife, Davada 'Dee' Stanley, who was then married to an Army sergeant stationed at Friedburg – Dee had telephoned Elvis to welcome him to Germany, and to offer her condolences on the death of his mother. Although she had picked up the telephone on the spur of the moment, and without knowing the Presley family, she was surprised when she was quickly connected with Elvis. He invited her to his hotel for coffee, but then found himself unable to meet her, and it was Vernon who stood in for him, after which Dee and Vernon became very close over the next few months. Almost inevitably, Elvis was rather put out that his father should have become emotionally involved with another woman so soon after Gladys had died, but to his credit, he seems to have kept his feelings to himself, and when Vernon and Dee told him of their plan to marry, he appeared to be pleased. Dee remembered that her future stepson said to her: 'Mrs. Stanley, I want my Daddy to be happy. He was a wonderful husband and father, and I've always wanted another brother – now I guess I'll have three (Dee had three young sons, Billy, Rick and David Stanley). We can just add another room to Graceland'.

Two other significant events occurred while Elvis was in Germany, which would have far-reaching effects on his future life. Through an Army friend named Rex Mansfield, he was introduced to the sport of karate, and took to it with enthusiasm, to the point where he had graduated to a second degree black belt by the time he left Germany. The fascination with this martial art would become an obsession after his return to the United States. The other event involved Presley's being introduced to the stimulating qualities of Dexedrine pills, which he was given by an Army sergeant as an artificial means of remaining awake during all-night manoeuvres. Elvis had always experienced trouble with sleep, both from the point of view of getting to sleep, and then with awakening from the effects of the sleeping pills he had taken. For the rest of his life, according to Red West, Elvis used Dexedrine when he wanted to stay awake.

In January 1960, Elvis was promoted to sergeant, and given a new job, commanding a three-man reconnaissance team of

Below left: Sergeant Presley in the Army mess hall.

Below: At an Army press conference relating to his discharge.

his own – his platoon leader noted: 'He earned the job, and I'll be glad to have him in my team at any time', typifying the lack of criticism directed at Elvis either by officers or fellow soldiers. He seems to have been a popular, hard-working soldier – as a spokesman remarked at the end of Elvis's tour of duty, 'There was a fierce loyalty that the other guys in the unit had for him, and I think it was because they sensed that he was a regular fellow. He sat in the snow with them, ate the lousy food, and the fact that he lived off the post and commuted in a fancy car didn't bother them. He would always get a lot of packages filled with cake and candy, more than he could eat, and he'd give it away. The other soldiers thought a lot of him'.

As soon as it was announced that Elvis would be discharged in early March 1960,

Colonel Parker began making plans for his return. Parker had not been idle while his 'boy' was away, and had kept the Elvis industry moving, making a lot of money in the process. Presley records had continued to sell well – each of the five very successful singles had sold more than one million copies, and some enterprising album repackaging had been undertaken despite the paucity of new material.

Among the 'new' albums was *A Date With Elvis*, released in September 1959, which featured a gatefold sleeve containing a photograph of Elvis in his Army uniform, a pictorial record of his departure for Germany, and a 1960 calendar. Of course, the contents of the album weren't new, with five tracks from the Sun days, plus songs from both 'Love Me Tender' and 'Jailhouse Rock', and a solitary pre-

Sergeant Presley leading his platoon through the snowy German streets.

viously unreleased item, *Is It So Strange*, but the lack of new material seemed to be of little concern to the fans, and the LP sold well. In Britain, incidentally, the track listing for *A Date With Elvis* was somewhat more expansive, with fourteen tracks as opposed to the ten on the American release, and a concentration on older material, but without the gatefold sleeve. At the end of 1959 came *50,000,000 Elvis Fans Can't Be Wrong*, another collection of *Greatest Hits*, whose sleeve featured Elvis in a remarkable gold lamé suit, that Colonel Parker had ordered from the famous Nudie of Hollywood.

Parker scanned the schedules for a suitable T.V. vehicle for Elvis's return, and discovered that Frank Sinatra was lining up his fourth and final T.V. special for ABC-T.V. The previous shows in the series had not performed particularly well in the ratings, and Sinatra was looking for a star name to attract more viewers – despite the fact that he had once described rock'n'roll as 'phony and false, sung, written and played by cretinous goons', Sinatra wanted Elvis, and agreed to pay Parker's huge fee of $125,000.

The first Elvis film of the 1960s was to be 'G.I. Blues', cleverly devised as a 'cash-in' on his stint in the Army. Producer Hal Wallis sent a crew to West Germany to shoot location footage, although taking care not to involve Elvis – as Wallis later noted 'We didn't want any criticism, and it might have been misunderstood in some quarters'. Meanwhile, 'Jailhouse Rock' was re-released and did excellent business in cinemas across the United States. At the same time, Freddie Bienstock was busy collecting demos of material for Elvis's first recording session of the new decade, several of the demos having been produced by a young man named Phil Spector, who would make a reputation for himself later in the 1960s as one of the all-time great record producers with artists like the Ronettes and the Crystals. A measure of the interest with which the public awaited Presley's return to recording was that RCA had taken over one million advance orders for a new single, at a time when not only was it not recorded, but the songs which would be on it had not even been selected – Elvis was returning to even greater popularity than he had experienced before the military hiatus.

Left: At the press reception given the day before his departure from Germany.

Below: On his way home after his German tour of duty.

He flew home to the United States on a DC-7 plane from Frankfurt on March 5, and among the crowd who turned out to wave him off at the airport was Priscilla Beaulieu. One magazine would later publish her photograph with the caption 'The girl he left behind', but it was the only publication to spot her, and no one else picked up the story. Elvis gave a press conference prior to his departure – where he was amazed to see former Sun Records employee Marion Keisker, who was now in the Army, working for Armed Forces Television – and also on his arrival at Fort Dix, New Jersey, where his plane landed in a blizzard. 'I learned a lot about people in the Army,' he told reporters, 'I never lived with people before and had a chance to find out how they think, and that changed me, but I can't tell you offhand how. If I'd been what they thought, I'd have got what was coming to me, but I never talked about show business.'

He returned to Memphis from New Jersey by train, and was then escorted back to Graceland by the police, after which he was quickly in touch with several old friends, who he reinstated on his personal payroll. Two Army colleagues, Charlie Hodge and Joe Esposito, joined his paid group of friends and assistants – Esposito was the only northerner, and a man who had impressed Elvis with his skill in financial matters, and who subsequently became the most trusted Graceland employee. Elvis also arranged for the purchase of a nearby house for Vernon and Dee, having changed his mind about them living at Graceland – while he wanted his father close at hand, he was unwilling for another woman to live in the house which had meant so much to his mother. Dee and Vernon were married in her home town of Huntsville, Alabama, on July 3, 1960, and although Elvis was due to attend the ceremony, he eventually didn't go, explaining that everywhere he went, things tended to get out of control and adding, 'I think a wedding should be a sacred thing'.

On March 20, he was back at RCA Studios in Nashville to cut the all-important new single, and to start work on a new studio album with the appropriate title of *Elvis Is Back!* Along with the Nashville studio musicians and D.J. Fontana, Scotty Moore also played on the

Opposite top: Coming home to Memphis with Colonel Parker, and (opposite bottom) the welcoming party at Graceland for the returning serviceman; (left to right) Earl Greenwood, one-time Fan Club President, singer Buddy Shepherd, Army comrade and longtime Presley associate Charlie Hodge, and (rear) Larry McCalla.

Left: Home at last and back in civvies; Elvis at a homecoming press conference.

A 1960 portrait.

session, and for the first time, a Presley session was recorded in stereo. The song chosen as the new single was *Stuck On You*, and when the record was released a few days after the session, advance orders had reached 1,275,077, while sales would eventually amount to well over two million copies. A second session in early April produced more tracks for the new album, plus the next two singles – *It's Now Or Never* held the Number One position on the chart for five weeks during the summer of 1960, while *Are You Lonesome Tonight* repeated the feat, but for six weeks, during November and December.

Elvis with Frank Sinatra, pictured during the latter's T.V. Special.

Elvis with another King – the King and Queen of Thailand, in fact – at Paramount Studios, June 1960.

Back in uniform for the filming of 'G.I. Blues'.

Opposite: Elvis standing proudly outside Graceland with his new Rolls-Royce.

These sessions produced some of Elvis's best-loved and biggest selling records – *Elvis Is Back!* was a twelve-track album (value for money in view of some of the shorter LPs previously released in Presley's name), with a strong collection of songs including few of the light and insubstantial items that had been used to pad out earlier LPs. He had undoubtedly made a special effort after two years away from the music scene, perhaps half-wondering whether the sceptics who had suggested he might no longer be able to make hit records could have been correct.

Any possible worries were proved groundless, and Elvis was still 'The King' – no one had surfaced to replace him, and the artists who had seemed to provide a threat when he went into the Army had met a variety of fates. Buddy Holly had died in an air crash, Little Richard had renounced his music in favour of becoming a preacher, Jerry Lee Lewis was in disgrace after a trip to Britain with his thirteen-year-old child bride/cousin, Chuck Berry was in prison, and Carl Perkins, Bill Haley and several others had simply lost their popular appeal and with it, the ability to make hit records. After the exciting days of the mid-1950s, there was a lull in popular music, which was short of both new stars and fresh trends, and as a result, Elvis was able to restart his career from a position right at the top.

He had, of course, changed significantly, partly on the advice of Colonel Parker, and partly because he was two years older and more experienced. He was also losing his rebellious looks and manner – he no longer wore such startling clothes, he didn't have long sideburns, and his frantic stage movements had become a thing of the past. Added to these visual changes, furious rock'n'roll songs were now largely excluded from his recording sessions, and most of the material was of a slower, more balladic type – *It's Now Or Never* was based on *O Sole Mio*, an Italian operetta piece, and *Are You Lonesome Tonight* had been written in the 1920s, and was part recitation – while Christmas 1960 saw the release of *His Hand In Mine*, an album of gospel songs recorded with the Jordanaires, which could be said to reveal his more serious side. The musicians with whom Elvis worked had also changed, and were gen-

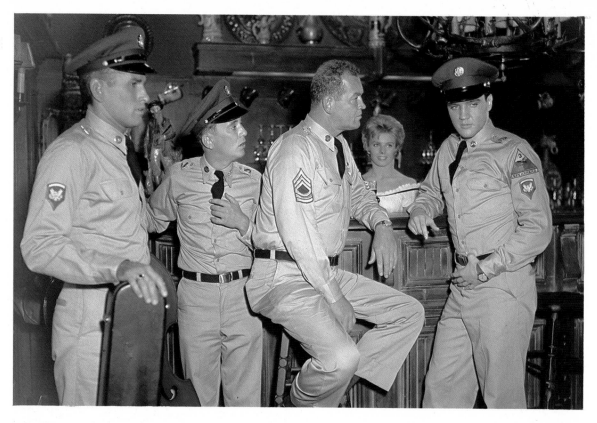

erally constituent parts of the successful 'Nashville Sound', and had perfected a much smoother and more mellow style, although Elvis had not completely turned his back on the past, and there was still a discernible rockabilly feel to some of his records, as where saxophonist 'Boots' Randolph added a vital kick to a couple of tracks on *Elvis Is Back!*

The rebellious days were also recalled by Elvis's role in the film, 'Flaming Star', but it proved to be one of his least successful, perhaps because few songs were featured, and also due to its serious subject matter. It was further proof for Colonel Parker and Presley's other busi-

ness associates that the correct path for Elvis to follow during the 1960s was for him to move towards becoming a 'middle-of-the-road' entertainer, and thereby appealing to the largest possible audience.

A taste of things to come was provided when Elvis made his first television appearance in several years, with Frank Sinatra, a hero of middle-aged music fans, and for which Elvis wore a tuxedo. After singing both sides of his latest single, Elvis joined Sinatra in a bizarre duet – Sinatra sang part of Elvis's hit *Love Me Tender*, and Elvis sang part of the Sinatra classic, *Witchcraft*, but the show overall was a major success, winning forty-one per cent of the viewing audience when it was screened on May 12, 1960. The Colonel began to tell anyone who asked that the price for Elvis appearing on television was now $150,000, an unprecedented fee for which there were no takers, but Parker was by no means upset, and said resolutely: 'I don't want Elvis to compete with his own movies' – he had decided that films were the perfect medium for Elvis' talents, as they could be screened all over the world, and were potentially huge money-spinners.

'G.I. Blues' starred Elvis as Tulsa McLean (a pseudonym more recently used by one of the better Presley imitators, Les Gray), an American soldier

Showering in 'G.I. Blues' – note the 'Fresh Fish Special' haircut.

stationed in West Germany who forms a musical group with two of his colleagues in an effort to make enough money to launch a night club when they are discharged from the Service. Elvis becomes involved in a bet to try to win the heart of a stand-offish cabaret dancer (played by Juliet Prowse), and is so successful that the couple genuinely fall in love. Most critics slammed the movie – 'Hollywood Reporter' noted 'It is a subdued and changed Elvis Presley who has returned to star in Hal Wallis' "G.I. Blues" – and for the majority of Elvis's rock'n'roll fans, the disappointing lack of good music (with two or three exceptions) and the sight of their hero playing with both puppets and children marked a complete sell-out.' However, it soon became clear that those who were disappointed were in a minority, as most people who saw the film apparently loved it, to the point where it became a box-office smash, grossing over four million dollars. A point of interest concerns one of the ballads featured in the film, *Wooden Heart*, which was based on a folk song, and which Elvis partially sang in German. It became a big hit in Europe, but RCA decided not to release it as a single in America, where-

upon another enterprising American label, Smash Records, recorded a cover version of the song featuring Elvis soundalike Joe Dowell, and scored a chart topping American hit.

'G.I. Blues' was released while Elvis was filming 'Flaming Star', a film that provided him with a rare chance to play a straight acting role and only included two fairly nondescript songs. The film was completed in around six weeks at the Conejo Ranch in the San Fernando Valley, where many popular T.V. western series are shot, and was directed by Don Siegel, who would later achieve fame for his work on a series of action films starring Clint Eastwood. Elvis played Pacer Burton, a half-breed whose loyalties are divided between the Kiowa Indians and the local white settlers, until they are polarized by the murder of his Indian mother.

Because it was rather less successful than his previous films, 'Flaming Star' spelt the end for straight acting roles – from now on, Elvis films would be filled with songs, although his third film of 1960, 'Wild In The Country', was made before this rule could be established, and apparently several songs which had originally been included were excised from the final print. Elvis took the part of Glenn Tyler in the film, Tyler being a simple country boy whose anti-social behaviour marks him down as a juvenile delinquent. Hope Lange plays a psychiatrist who tries to steer Elvis back to the straight and narrow, Tuesday Weld is a young and sexy miscreant determined to lead Elvis back to his wicked ways, and Millie Perkins plays his childhood sweetheart, selflessly urging him to behave and to get a proper college education. The film is not remembered as one of Presley's best.

Colonel Tom Parker was pleased at the way things had proceeded since Elvis's return from the Army, and decided that his client should continue to star in three films each year. Each movie would open to the general public during a school vacation, thus allowing the Elvis family audience the maximum opportunity to see them as often as they wished. Side by side with a regular pattern of record releases – four singles and three albums annually – it seemed the perfect way to maintain Elvis's successful career for many years to come.

Opposite top: Delivering a coup de grâce *in 'Wild In The Country'.*

Opposite bottom: A tense exchange in 'Flaming Star'.

Left: 'O.K. Who took my shirt?' – a still from 'Flaming Star'.

THE CELLULOID HERO

During February and March 1961, Elvis gave his last concert performances for several years, including two shows in Memphis for the benefit of local charities such as the new St. Jude Children's Research Hospital, which Elvis supported extensively during the 1960s. Another was a major event which was staged at Pearl Harbour in Hawaii, co-starring film actor James Stewart and country comedienne Minnie Pearl, to raise money for a memorial to the U.S.S. *Arizona*, an American warship sunk by the Japanese during the Second World War. Gordon Stoker of the Jordanaires, who was involved with the Pearl Harbour show, recalled that Elvis gave a particularly impressive performance during a set of

Elvis with Joan Blackman, his co-star in 'Blue Hawaii', snapped in the grounds of the Hilton Hotel, Hawaii, during location shooting for the movie.

seventeen of his best-known songs, ending with the ever-popular *Hound Dog*. The vast majority of the recordings made at this show appeared on record for the first time in 1980 as part of an eight-LP set released as a limited edition to commemorate the twenty-fifth anniversary of Elvis singing with RCA Records.

Little did most of those at the Bloch Arena on March 25 suspect that it would be 1968 before Elvis stood before another live audience. After the concert, he remained in Hawaii to shoot authentic location footage for his next film, 'Blue Hawaii', although he would be concentrating his film-making in Hollywood in the future, mainly working for Paramount, Metro-Goldwyn-Mayer and United Artists.

In seven years Elvis made twenty-one films – which amounted to almost the total of his appearances in public, as he was not seen on television during this period, and rarely showed himself outside Graceland. When he wasn't either filming or working on the battery of soundtrack albums that comprised most of his recorded output during this time, he was apparently closeted with friends and associates behind the high walls of his Memphis mansion or in rented homes in California, leading an exceptionally private life and becoming increasingly separated from the outside world.

There were in fact only a handful of recording sessions at the RCA studio in Nashville unconnected with his movies, and these were to cut singles or so-called 'bonus' tracks for the soundtrack albums. Most of the best of these occurred in 1961, and yielded hits like *His Latest Flame*, *Little Sister* and *Good Luck Charm*, but from 1962 virtually every session took place in Los Angeles, and were designed

A torrid, but damp, love scene with Joan Blackman in 'Blue Hawaii'.

The wedding scene from 'Blue Hawaii'.

exclusively for the purpose of recording songs for the soundtracks of Elvis's movies. RCA were quite content on a commercial basis – whether they were as happy aesthetically is not recorded – as movies seemed to be the best advertisement for Presley's records, since he could be seen performing most new releases on cinema screens around the world. As films starring Elvis attracted huge audiences, substantial international promotion, and therefore sales, seemed to be more or less guaranteed.

The musicians who played on Presley records changed very little, and a regular team, including Scotty Moore, D.J. Fontana and Floyd Cramer, along with the Jordanaires and Chet Atkins, continued to be involved, although this now necessitated travelling to Los Angeles from time to time. March 1961 saw them working at Radio Recorders studio in Hollywood on the soundtrack to 'Blue Hawaii'. This featured fourteen songs, the best of which were an excellent ballad, *Can't Help Falling In Love*, and a more spirited effort, *Rock-A-Hula Baby*. Although in truth the music was fairly half-hearted in comparison with Elvis's earlier work, the soundtrack album eventually sold over five million copies, making it his all-time biggest-selling LP.

The film, whose advertising proclaimed that it included 'ecstatic romance, exotic

dances and exciting music', was a phenomenal box-office success. Elvis played Chad Gates, who returns to Hawaii after two years in the Army to find that his mother (Angela Lansbury) wants him to settle down, marry, and work in the family pineapple business. Elvis, of course, has other ideas, and becomes a tourist guide, as he enjoys showing pretty girls around the island, even though his steady girl-friend (played by Joan Blackman), who also works at the tourist bureau, is very jealous of the way he carries on with the visitors. The film ends with Elvis and Joan getting married at a colourful Hawaiian wedding party – the predictable happy ending.

'Blue Hawaii' became so popular that many subsequent Elvis films were modelled along very similar lines – each would feature an exotic location, pretty girls, several songs, with Elvis as a likeable and

Above: Elvis and Anne Helm on the set of 'Follow That Dream'.

Left: Elvis meets film director Elia Kazan in Hollywood.

Elvis jokingly menaces the Colonel on the set of 'Follow That Dream'.

easy-going character, although with a temper and willing to use his fists if provoked. He was usually cast as working in an unconventional (and, some might say, unlikely) job such as trapeze artist, racing driver, pop star or rodeo rider (the common factor of all these examples being that they are essentially glamorous).

The first Presley film of 1962 was 'Follow That Dream' released in time for that year's Easter holiday and featuring Elvis as Toby Kwimper, who runs a fishing business with his father, Pop Kwimper, played by Arthur O'Connell.

Pop is looking after three unofficially adopted children and an older girl named Holly, played by Ann Helm, who is Elvis's love interest.

The sketchy plot deals with the opening of a gambling club, as a result of which the local people are upset, and appoint Elvis as sheriff. The gangsters who profit from the gambling try to pulverize Elvis in a fight, but using the martial arts skill he had learned in the Army, he fights them off. More trouble comes when a prying state welfare department superintendent decides that Pop's adopted family should be taken into care, but Elvis and his father contest the move in court, Elvis himself proving to be particularly eloquent, and the case is thrown out. Curiously, the film contained only four songs – the best of which by far was the title track – which were released as an EP shortly after the film's première.

The first (and only) non-soundtrack album of 1962, *Pot Luck With Elvis*, was on the whole uninspired, as were so many of his films during this period, and despite the promising inclusion of four songs written by ace New York songsmiths Doc Pomus and Mort Shuman, only one of the dozen tracks on the LP, *Suspicion*, was especially memorable. In many ways this

Signing autographs at a Florida aquashow at Weekie Wachee Springs.

was hardly surprising as there was much more film work to be fitted in during the year – the second 1962 Presley movie was 'Kid Galahad' a remake of a 1937 film starring Edward G. Robinson, Bette Davis and Humphrey Bogart, and the posters proclaimed: 'Presley packs the screen's biggest wallop . . . with the girls . . . with the gloves . . . with the guitar.' Elvis played a tough, if not very talented boxer, who is able to take a lot of punishment. He is exploited by his manager, played by Gig Young, who needs money to pay off gambling debts owed to a crook (David Lewis). Joan Blackman, again featured as Elvis's girl, is also his manager's daughter. One unpleasant scene occurs when Elvis's trainer (played by Charles Bronson) has his fingers broken for refusing to fix a big fight, but then Elvis, followed by a repentant Gig Young, arrives to deal with the crooks. Elvis decides to forsake the world of pugilism for a career in the motor trade, and of course marries Joan Blackman.

Although the film's plot was superior to many other Elvis movie vehicles during this period, the music, about half a dozen songs released as an EP, was below par, and if the EP had not been sandwiched between two Top Five singles, *She's Not*

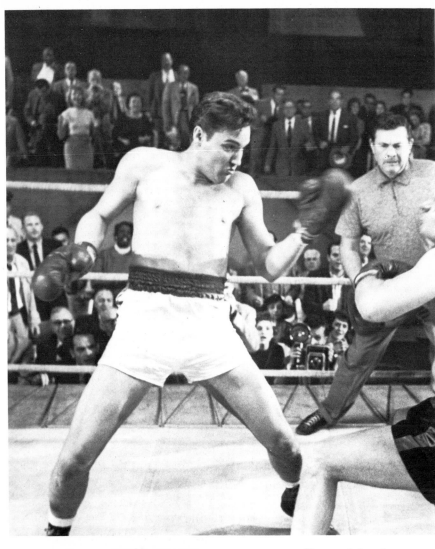

Above: A knockout punch from Elvis in 'Kid Galahad'.

Left: Joan Blackman leading Elvis to the altar in the same film.

Three contrasting stills from 'Girls! Girls! Girls!', 1962.

You and *Return To Sender*, the public might have been forgiven for supposing that Elvis was losing his way.

Return To Sender was, in fact, the best song to be featured in his next film, 'Girls! Girls! Girls!', which was released for Christmas, 1962. In it, Elvis starred as the poverty-stricken captain of a charter boat, who sings in a nightclub each evening to earn enough money to purchase his craft outright. He meets Laurel Dodge (played by Laurel Goodwin), who is rich, but pretends to be poor, and falls for Elvis, for whom she secretly buys the boat he wants. He is most annoyed when he discovers the

truth, as he will not accept charity from anyone, and makes her sell the boat again, whereupon he sets about building his own craft.

Despite the fact that many of the usual crew were involved, including Scotty, D.J., Boots Randolph and the Jordanaires, who were augmented by notable Los Angeles session stars like guitarist Barney Kessel and drummer Hal Blaine, the overall lack of quality to be found in the thirteen songs in the soundtrack (with the exception of the excellent *Return To Sender*) was typified by the ludicrous *Song Of The Shrimp*, used in the film as fisherman Elvis serenades his catch.

Unconventional fan photos from the early 1960s – note Vernon Presley in bottom picture.

Colonel Tom Parker, who was credited in every Presley movie as Technical Adviser, kept a watch on each one's preparation and made sure that in his opinion, sufficient songs were included, regardless of whether or not songs were strictly necessary for the storyline. He was given an office within the Paramount studio complex in Hollywood, and later had one at M.G.M. That he had managed to acquire these premises rent free as part of Elvis's contract was typical of the man, and he was never afraid to ask for extra benefits which, as he was Presley's manager, were usually supplied. For example, he had several assistants, but only Tom Diskin received a salary from the Colonel, the rest being paid by either Paramount or RCA.

Parker's office was filled with Presley mementoes – the cardboard jail from 'Jailhouse Rock' stood in one corner, and there were numerous posters and film stills, making it an appropriate place from which to co-ordinate each film's publicity. The Colonel also looked after all his client's business affairs, and kept people away from Elvis, including the press: 'Holding interviews with only a select few is making enemies of all the rest,' he said when announcing that Elvis would no longer talk to press reporters. 'It isn't fair to designate a handful of people and have you talk to only them.'

This policy created an exclusive air around Elvis, although the reason for the ploy was to prevent Elvis saying something that might hurt his image – in one unguarded moment, when a reporter enquired why he hadn't married, Elvis replied, 'Why buy apples when you live in

97

an orchard?', a comment which the Colonel realized could easily lose the support Elvis had gained from adults he had impressed during his time in the Army.

While he was filming in Hollywood, Elvis rented houses in the exclusive and expensive Bel Air district of Los Angeles, spending nearly five years at 565 Perugia Way, a short spell in a huge mansion at 1059 Bellagio Road, and eighteen months at a ranch-style home at 10550 Rocca Place, close by the Bel Air Hotel, but Graceland remained his only real home, as he explained to a reporter before the interview embargo: 'It isn't that I don't like Hollywood, but a man gets lonesome for the things that are familiar to him, like friends and acquaintances. That's why I would never live in Hollywood permanently, although it's a lovely city, and I've learned to appreciate it a lot since we moved into a Mediterranean-style villa that I rent on a hilltop in Bel Air. It's so quiet there, and the place is all marble columns and statues – it's a fine home, but home for me will always spell Memphis and Graceland.'

The Hollywood film crowd tried to involve Elvis in their social scene, but he remained seemingly aloof, and Stan Brossette, the film company press officer who had the difficult job of fending off numerous requests for interviews and photo sessions, recalled: 'He was always a guest, never a constant figure in Hollywood – he just came to the studio, did his work and then left. The producers always tried to convince me that I should bring him along to parties, but he never came – he brought his own party from Memphis along.'

Presley's friends from Memphis, then tagged El's Angels because of their habit of riding powerful Harley-Davidson motorcycles along the wide streets of Memphis after midnight, went with him everywhere, including the film sets, to keep him company and participate in games, like water pistol and shaving foam fights, to relieve boredom. Marty Lacker explained in the book 'Portrait Of A Friend': 'All this may sound childish, but it was an essential part of the life-style of a group of guys who were doing things day in and day out – we had to let off steam'.

The men who worked for Elvis found that the job had both distinct advantages

and disadvantages – on the plus side were the frequent parties, a steady flow of very pretty girls eager to meet someone who could help them get close to Elvis, a roof over their heads, and free food and drink, but from the other aspect, they had to contend with long hours, being 'on call' twenty-four hours a day, a severely disrupted life and poor pay. Alan Fortas, who looked after Elvis's travelling arrangements, told Jerry Hopkins 'We had a kind of fast turnover – they'd quit, leave, come back, and some of the boys worked for Elvis three or four different times'. However, among those who stayed longest with Elvis were Lamar Fike, a fat man who was frequently the butt of Elvis's practical jokes; Red West, who was a stunt man in several Presley movies, and was regularly knocked about by his boss as a result; and Marvin Gamble, who doubled as chauffeur and valet – each member of the Presley entourage had a specific job, aside from providing companionship whenever it was required.

The Memphis Mafia, as they became known, did everything they were asked, following Elvis's instructions implicitly, rarely disagreeing with or criticizing any-

thing he did, however crazy or foolish they might consider it. If Elvis conceived a madcap scheme, they followed it, if he wanted to take up a new sport, they all played, and if he had the urge to see the same film several times, they watched too. In Bel Air, Elvis's friends organized frequent parties for their boss, when they were invariably outnumbered by attractive young girls, but in Memphis, social activities tended to involve predominantly male company, and included late-night motorcycle rides and games of American football with no holds barred as well as other bizarre activities inside Graceland. One popular game apparently involved throwing hundreds of photographic flash cubes into the swimming pool, then shooting at them with BB guns – as each one was hit, it exploded dramatically before sinking to the bottom, and this activity is said to have kept Elvis and his friends happy for hours.

Fewer outsiders were invited to Graceland, and one reason for this was that from May 1962, Priscilla Beaulieu was living there. Elvis had remained besotted by the young girl after his return from West Germany, telephoning her regularly and,

with help from Dee and Minnie Mae Presley, had arranged for her to visit Graceland at Christmas 1960. On her return, Elvis made frequent calls to her stepfather, Joseph Beaulieu, trying to persuade him to allow Priscilla to live at Graceland, to which Beaulieu eventually agreed, providing that she lived with Vernon and Dee at their house on Dolan Street (which backed on to Graceland), and that they became virtual guardians.

As Priscilla had not completed her schooling, she was enrolled at the Immaculate Conception High School for Catholic girls in Memphis. After graduating on June 14, 1963, she attended the Patricia Stevens Finishing and Career School where she studied dancing and modelling. Because Elvis was away in Hollywood for long periods, Priscilla spent a lot of time with Vernon, Dee and Minnie Mae. According to Dee, in the book 'Elvis: We Love You Tender', 'she did things that most normal teenagers do, except when Elvis was home, when she would do the things he wanted to do – parties, movies, riding. But she wasn't in any way a normal teenager, because it was always assumed that one day she and Elvis would get

Above left: Disc jockey Jimmy Savile (pre-O.B.E.) presenting Elvis with a gold disc for a million sales of It's Now Or Never, Hollywood, 1962.

Above: The late Albert Hand, founder and editor of 'Elvis Monthly', and his wife Phyllis meet their hero, 1962.

married'. Dee seems to feel that Elvis was testing Priscilla during this time, to see if she would be able to cope with the pressure that would inevitably accrue for Mrs. Elvis Presley – as Dee noted: 'She came to Graceland to see how we lived and what we really expected, and she proved that she could stay there with the family – pass the test, so to speak – and she did really well. She was everything he wanted'.

Until 1963, Elvis's films and records were very popular and he remained very much The King, with every single and LP reaching the Top Ten in the chart and the movies proving to be box-office attractions, but a change was coming. Playing safe had become the keynote of Elvis's career, and his erstwhile fans gradually began to tire of the over-familiar story lines in each film, not to mention the songs, which increasingly sounded like retreads of earlier hits. The formula that had worked so well in 'Blue Hawaii' was overstretched, and the use of the same musicians and especially the same songwriters (in particular Sid Tepper and Roy Bennett, a Brill building writing partnership who provided little that was exceptional for Elvis, although they did provide big hits for Britain's Elvis equivalent, Cliff Richard, in the shape of *Travellin' Light* and *The Young Ones*, among others) meant that the songs sounded more and more alike, while it was becoming increasingly clear that less care and attention was being lavished both on the songs and the way they were recorded, without it being possible for anyone to pinpoint precisely why they were inferior.

Elvis was slowly declining in popularity, although his earning capacity was not impaired, as thanks to the shrewd business dealing of the Colonel, more money was being made even though less product was sold and fewer cinema seats were filled. For some movies, Elvis received an advance of a cool million dollars against fifty per cent of the profits! To outside observers, it seemed ludicrous for Elvis to continue making trashy films that lacked substance and to record inferior songs, but he was making so much money that changing direction became increasingly difficult. As 'Flaming Star' director Don Siegel once remarked, 'I believe he just went along with those things because he was so successful and made so much money'.

Many critics have tended to write off the work Elvis produced between 1963 and the summer of 1968 as worthless, and while most of the films were undeniably disappointing, several good records by Elvis were released during this period, including *(You're The) Devil In Disguise*, *Viva Las Vegas*, *Such A Night*, *Ain't That Loving You Baby*, *Crying In The Chapel* and *Little Egypt*. While many other songs were weak and the musical backing uninspired for much of the time, Elvis's own performances were anything but routine – as rock writer Dave Marsh has pointed out, 'He seized each song that possessed a glimmer of worth and wrung out its full potential'.

The decline was visible and audible with the first Presley movie of 1963, 'It Happened At The World's Fair', which included ten songs, all of them brief, adding up to a total running time of just over twenty minutes. Even the single from the film, *One Broken Heart For Sale*, lasted a mere one minute thirty four seconds, and significantly peaked at Number 11 in the charts, becoming his first record to miss the Top Ten since 1956. The film seemed more like a travelogue advertising the World's Fair at Seattle, Washington, than a real movie, and featured Elvis and Gary Lockwood as pilots whose plane had been seized by a sheriff. The plot complications included smugglers and Presley's involvement with two females, a nurse played by Joan O'Brien, and a Chinese child played by Vicky Tiu whom he accompanies around the Fair.

Critics suggested that the music in 'Fun In Acapulco', the second Elvis film release of 1963, was noticeably improved, as every track possessed a suitably Mexican flavour. The best song, *Bossa Nova Baby*, written by Leiber and Stoller, returned Elvis to the Top Ten after the relative failure of *One Broken Heart For Sale*, and apparently several tracks from the LP were successful when released as singles in Central America. This was the film in which Elvis played a trapeze artist, Mike Windgren, who comes to the holiday playground of Acapulco after a terrifying high wire accident in which his partner has been badly hurt. Working as a singer-cum-lifeguard(!), he becomes romanti-

Above: With Vicky Tiu in 'It Happened At The World's Fair'.

Left: As trapeze artist Mike Windgren in 'Fun In Acapulco'.

cally involved with a hotel social director, played by Ursula Andress, and finally overcomes his phobia about heights, which had been caused by the accident, with a dive of 136 feet from a cliff face.

Next came filming for 'Viva Las Vegas', although this was not to be the next Presley movie released, this 'privilege' being reserved for 'Kissin' Cousins'. 'Viva Las Vegas' (retitled 'Love In Las Vegas' in Britain) starred Elvis as a motor-racing ace named Lucky Jordan, who is in Las Vegas for an important race, but whose car is experiencing mechanical faults. He falls for Ann-Margret, the curvacious swimming instructress at a local hotel, succeeds in repairing his car and (no surprise for regular Presley film buffs) wins the race and the girl, also finding time to slot in a number of songs, although on this occasion, no soundtrack LP was released. Only one single coupling *Viva Las Vegas* and *What'd I Say* (the Ray Charles classic) plus an EP were released while the film was current, although several other tracks appeared on later compilation albums.

There was frequent speculation in newspaper gossip columns about Elvis and his involvement with his cinematic leading ladies, although most of them were incorrect, as he had little to do with other actors and actresses in his films. However, he did have a relationship with Ann-Margret during the making of 'Viva Las Vegas', and for once spent time socializing away from his Bel Air home. Priscilla heard the stories – Ann-Margret reportedly mentioned possible wedding plans – and temporarily moved away from Graceland to stay with her parents, who by that time had returned to the United States and were living in San Francisco, but the affair seems to have been brief, and before long, Priscilla was back in Memphis.

'Kissin' Cousins', which was released a few weeks before 'Viva Las Vegas' despite being made subsequently, set new low standards for Elvis films, and was produced by Sam Katzman, who had a reputation in Hollywood as 'king of the quickies'. Lance LeGault, who was responsible for choreography in several

Presley films, told Jerry Hopkins: 'We shot 'Kissin' Cousins'' in seventeen days, and I think that film was the turning point in Presley films – up until that time, certain standards had been maintained, but that was where we noticed that there was no rehearsal for all the numbers'.

The movie featured Elvis in two roles – as Josh Morgan, an air force officer trying to persuade a family of rural folk to sell their land for a government missile site, and as Jodie Tatum, one of the locals who resents the intrusion. The soundtrack LP seemed to lack even one redeeming feature.

The final film of 1964, 'Roustabout', cast Elvis (or so the publicity had it) as a 'roving, restless, reckless roustabout'. He played the part of karate expert Charlie Rogers, who joins the travelling carnival owned by Maggie Morgan, played by Barbara Stanwyck, and attracts large crowds with his singing. Any similarity with other Elvis films which the reader may discern continues – he falls for another carnival employee, played by Joan Freeman, but then leaves the show after a fight. Barbara Stanwyck faces bankruptcy without Elvis's ability as an entertainer, so Joan follows him and begs him to return. Although the soundtrack album's generally mundane qualities were only relieved by the Leiber/Stoller classic, *Little Egypt*, it still sold sufficiently well to top the American LP charts, his first Number One album for a while and significantly, his last during the 1960s, bearing in mind that it was released during the first quarter of 1964.

It cannot be denied that the quality of Elvis's films declined still further during the next year, 1965 – critics could not find a kind word to say about them, and even devoted fans were evidently losing interest, to the point where one fan wrote to the English magazine, 'Elvis Monthly', and described the films as 'puppet shows for not overbright children'. At least vintage Elvis fans might have enjoyed his 1964 Christmas single, which coupled the 1957 recording of *Blue Christmas* with *Wooden Heart*, but the quite awful 'Girl Happy', the first film of the new year, remains significant only because it contains some of the most ridiculous songs Elvis would ever record. Even the Beatles (by this time the biggest act in the world)

Left: Elvis and his wife to be, Priscilla Beaulieu, before they were married, captured on film by Elvis's Uncle Vester.

Left: With Barbara Stanwyck on the set of 'Roustabout', and (below) Elvis, Barbara Stanwyck (left) and Joan Freeman test the fairground equipment in the same film.

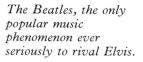
Off duty in the recording studio, 1965.

The Beatles, the only popular music phenomenon ever seriously to rival Elvis.

might not have got away with *Fort Lauderdale Chamber Of Commerce* or the film's single, *Do The Clam*, but Elvis evidently did, and despite the justified sneers from critics, a substantial audience was still turning out to see his films, guaranteeing a healthy profit. Elvis was by now the highest paid entertainer in Hollywood, although his remuneration was in diametric opposition to the entertainment his films provided. 'Elvis invades bikini country' proclaimed the posters for 'Girl Happy', in which Elvis is

hired by nightclub owner Harold Stone to chaperone his mischievous daughter, Shelley Fabares, on a holiday in Florida. Shelley provides Elvis with many problems, and at one point, he has to tunnel beneath a prison to rescue her. Aside from the insubstantial songs, the film displays some unusual and unnatural Florida scenery – at one point, the normally flat state is seen to have grown mountains!

At least there was some consolation for Elvis fans later in the year with the release of a single of *Crying In The Chapel*, a 1960 recording in which Elvis covered a 1950s hit for Sonny Til and the Orioles. The single reached the Top Three in the United States, and in Britain became his first chart topper for two years (and his last before 1970), but the release of the next film, 'Tickle Me', seemed to undo any good achieved by the release of a track from the archives. The film's reviewer in the 'New York Times' was typical of the critical response, writing: 'This is the silliest, feeblest and dullest vehicle for the Memphis wonder in a long time', and when it was premièred during the summer of 1965, it seemed to mark another all-time low. Elvis plays a rodeo rider who finds himself working as a handyman at an expensive health farm for women, and the plot involves a treasure map, a ghost town, the inevitable crooks, English actress Jocelyn Lane as Elvis's girlfriend, and a number of songs left over from other films or reused from already released albums.

Despite the depths to which Elvis's career had plunged, many fans continued to hold him in high regard, although more on the strength of his early achievements than anything he had accomplished more recently, and among those who still regarded him as The King were the four Beatles, who visited him in his Bel Air retreat on the evening of August 27, 1965.

As the biggest popular music phenomenon since Elvis had burst on the scene in the mid-1950s, the Beatles had spearheaded an 'English Invasion' of the American charts, supported by other popular groups like the Rolling Stones, the Animals and Herman's Hermits, the result of which was that many American acts were being effectively barred from the upper reaches of their own Hot 100.

Colonel Parker, who was well aware of the importance of these young pretenders, had sent a telegram from himself and Elvis to welcome the Beatles to 'The Ed Sullivan Show' on the night when they surpassed Presley's own record share of the viewing audience, established in 1957, and also sent them each a smart cowboy suit, complete with six-shooters. The Beatles were most impressed, and when they arrived in Los Angeles to play the Hollywood Bowl, their manager, Brian Epstein, arranged a summit meeting – as John Lennon said later, 'There was only one person in the United States that we really wanted to meet' – and their four hours together, between 10.000 p.m. and 2.00 a.m., included some conversation about recording, plus a brief jam session, which cannot have been recorded, or it would undoubtedly have subsequently surfaced. The Liverpudlians revealed themselves to be enthusiastic Elvis fans, but equally made no secret of their disdain for his latter-day records – when John Lennon asked why Elvis didn't make records in his old style, the answer was that it was mainly due to his intensive film schedule, although Elvis did add that he might make an old-style record 'for kicks'. Whereupon Lennon enthusiastically exclaimed 'We'll buy it!'

There were many fans who agreed with

the Beatles in wishing that Elvis would revert to Sun-style rock'n'roll records, but they would have to be patient until 1968, when he returned to his old sound during a T.V. special. At this point in 1965 Elvis was stuck on a treadmill, apparently having grown to loathe the movies he was making, but being unable to stop because contracts had been signed, the money was so good and the Colonel had decreed that he should continue.

The mid-1960s passed in a haze for Elvis and those around him, to some extent because he had become dependent on various pills. Still suffering from insomnia, he took sleeping tablets, but found it necessary to neutralize their effects by taking 'uppers' which would wake him in time for early starts in film schedules. His aides have subsequently revealed that he took large quantities of drugs, always describing them as 'medication' (a favourite rock star expression which cloaks illegal substances with a trace of supposed legal approval) and checking their effects in 'The Physician's Desk Reference', a tome which accompanied him everywhere. However, no one seems to have felt strongly enough about Elvis's drug intake to suggest that he be less extravagant – everyone did what they thought he wanted, and if he chose to take so many pills, they saw no reason to put their necks on the line by recommending him to curtail his habits.

All his associates considered their employer's eating habits strange, but for the same reason, no one appears to have criticized him. According to Marty Lacker, 'There was a phase in Los Angeles when he ate meat loaf, mashed potatoes, gravy and sliced tomatoes every night, and when he ate hamburgers, they had to be extra, extra well done, almost burned, with onions, pickles and mustard'. This unusual diet made Elvis gain weight, which worried him, and he would go for

days on end when he would eat very little, until, starving from his fast, he would go on an eating binge, gorging himself with food. His diet and attempts to control it provoked strange moods in Elvis, and his temper would occasionally flare up, sometimes leading him to fire his aides, only to recall them later in a fit of remorse.

Exiled from the outside world and living with no one but totally subservient employees, it comes as no real surprise to discover that the Presley life-style became increasingly and dangerously bizarre, although it never became obvious to outsiders, and was certainly never evident in his films, in which he always appeared to be exactly the same, typifying the easy-going, fun-loving, all-American male.

'Harum Scarum', the final 1965 movie, was advertised as '1001 swingin' nights, as Elvis brings the big beat to Baghdad in a riotous, rockin', rollin' adventure spoof!' While the copywriter involved was certainly a master of alliteration, the plot, in which Elvis as pop star Johnny Tyronne is kidnapped in the Middle East, possessed hardly any credibility at all. After complications and the attempted murder of a king, whose life is predictably enough saved by Elvis, plus appearances by many pretty girls and a gang of thieves, Tyronne is able to return to America with a

princess, played by Mary Ann Mobley, and a troupe of belly dancers who enliven his Las Vegas routine.

Rumours that the entire project, including the recording of the eminently disposable soundtrack album, were completed in under three weeks seem entirely feasible, and this is considered by many critics to be the absolute nadir of Presley's film career, a view which the soundtrack LP unfortunately only supports.

1966 would see Elvis's record sales also plummeting, although this decline was only relative and represented an inability to reach the Top Ten, a height to which very few acts ever aspire but which, for Elvis, spelt a slump. The year's three films provided no solace – the first, 'Frankie and Johnny', portrayed Elvis as an inveterate gambler, and Donna Douglas as his girlfriend, Frankie. The couple are singers on a Mississippi showboat and part of their act is the famous 'Frankie and Johnny' story. One night, a genuine bullet is slipped into Donna's gun, and she really shoots Elvis, who appears to be dead, but is in fact merely stunned, as the bullet has struck his lucky charm. In an attempt to stimulate falling sales of Elvis's soundtrack albums, which had once sold in vast quantities, RCA included a bonus with the *Frankie And Johnny* LP in the shape of a full colour portrait of the star, but were rewarded with only a brief spell in the Top 20.

As box office receipts were also falling, Paramount made their most blatant attempt to repeat the success of 'Blue Hawaii' by returning to the same island locations for 'Paradise – Hawaiian Style',

Left: Elvis with Donna Douglas in 'Frankie And Johnny' and (below) one of the showboat routines from the same film.

but as it was such a pale imitation, it was regarded as little better than 'Harum Scarum' – Elvis runs a helicopter service in Hawaii, but one day temporarily loses control of his machine, forcing a driver off the road. The angry driver turns out to be an official of the Federal Aviation Agency, and Presley is forbidden to fly, but when he hears that his partner has crash landed, he rushes to the rescue, ignoring the fact that the resulting publicity may prevent him ever regaining his licence to fly. Fortunately, the F.A.A. official has a forgiving nature, and everyone lives happily ever after.

The nine songs by Elvis on the soundtrack album include *It's A Dog's Life*, which probably summed up Elvis's feelings about his film career at the time – when the regular movie-making days were over, he would confess 'It was getting harder and harder singing to the camera all day long. Let's face it, when you have ten different songs for each movie, they can't all be good – eventually, I just got tired of singing to turtles and the guys I'd just beaten up!'

The only constructive recordings of the year took place around the time that 'Paradise – Hawaiian Style' was released, and marked Elvis's return to the recording studio for a non-cinematic project after a gap of three years. As well as cutting tracks for a religious LP, *How Great Thou Art*, which was released in early 1967, two meaningful singles, *Love Letters* and *Indescribably Blue*, were also released, although the public were by now evidently unwilling to purchase even above-average Presley records in sufficient quantities to place them in the U.S. Top Ten, and the end of the year saw a return to mediocre movies with 'Spinout', which a harassed publicity copy writer described as 'Elvis with his foot on the gas and no brakes on the fun'. Playing a racing driver/pop star, Elvis is preparing to drive an experimental car in a big race, and is chased by three girls, Shelley Fabares, who is a spoilt rich girl, Diane McBain, a best-selling authoress who is researching a book with the title 'The Perfect American Male', and Deborah Walley, who is the drummer in Elvis's band. The film soundtrack contained the first film songs that might possibly be described as 'rock' since his film 'Girl Happy' nearly four years earlier.

The first 1967 film 'Easy Come, Easy Go' starred Elvis as a frogman who discovers what appears to be a treasure chest while exploring an underwater wreck. The rightful owner, a disco dancer and yoga enthusiast played by Dodie

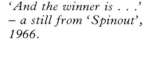

'And the winner is . . .' – a still from 'Spinout', 1966.

Marshall, helps Elvis to recover the treasure, with the proviso that any proceeds will be used to help the local arts centre, but some crooks hear about the treasure and manage to procure the chest first. Elvis chases them, only to discover that the supposed treasure actually consists of almost valueless copper coins. The six-track EP of songs from the film was equally worthless. Shortly before this was released, the religious LP *How Great Thou Art* was released. It was largely recorded during the previous year, but contained also *Crying In The Chapel* from a late 1960 session. It stands as Elvis's finest recording during the mid-1960s, despite its less than strictly commercial approach.

An even more significant event occurred on May 1, 1967, when Elvis and Priscilla were finally married in Las Vegas, although his still-crowded filming schedule allowed rather less time for a honeymoon than was appropriate for a 'King' – 'Double Trouble' was about to be released, and 'Clambake' wasn't quite finished. Although the plot of 'Double Trouble' took Elvis to England, the entire film was shot in a Hollywood studio, and conceivably the British aspect was one of the very few concessions made by Elvis to the changing musical fashions of the time, another being the inclusion of a Bob Dylan song, *Tomorrow Is A Long Time*, as a 'bonus track' on the 'Spinout' soundtrack LP.

Above left: With Linda Wong in 'Paradise – Hawaiian Style'.

Above: Discovering the joy of yoga in 'Easy Come, Easy Go'.

Left: A moody still from 'Double Trouble'.

In 'Double Trouble' Elvis plays a singer in a club who romances Annette Day, but her father is angered by the relationship and sends his daughter away to school in Belgium to prevent her seeing Elvis. By complete (and completely unlikely) coincidence, Elvis happens to have a booking in Brussels, and the couple are soon reunited, but then plunge into an adventure involving jewel smuggling. Although Presley's cinematic English backing band sported Beatle-style long hair, the music in the film was far from typical of the quality of contemporary British music, and such tracks as *Old MacDonald* (the same interminable chorus song incorporating animal noises) and *Long Legged Girl (With The Short Dress On)* were particularly bad. As Dave Marsh wrote in his book 'Elvis': 'Who could sing such drool and make it stick? Who could put across such drivel and keep the customers lined up for more? Only Elvis.'

Fortunately, the end of Presley's conveyor-belt film schedule was almost in sight. Even Colonel Parker realized that the movies were earning increasingly smaller profits, and that a change was vital if Elvis was to retain any credibility as a performer. Even so, existing contracts had to be honoured and several more films were lined up, the first of which was 'Clambake', with Elvis as a rich boy pretending to be poor, who changes places with a water-ski instructor, but then falls for Shelley Fabares (making her third starring appearance in Presley films) who is on the lookout for a rich husband. She also has eyes for Bill Bixby (now the human half of 'The Incredible Hulk' on television), a wealthy power-boat racer, so Elvis also gets involved with power boats, devises a miracle hardening agent that protects boats travelling at high speed, and ends up winning the race and the girl. Despite the dross that had preceded it, the *Clambake* soundtrack LP peaked at forty-seven in the album charts, marking yet another new low point, although it actually included two genuinely excellent bonus tracks in *Guitar Man* and *Big Boss Man*.

RCA Records, and even Colonel Parker, were fast losing faith in soundtrack albums, and the first of the 1968 films 'Stay Away Joe' included only a handful of songs, one of which, *Dominic*,

was a serenade sung by Elvis to a bull, and is so bad that it has never been released on record. The film purported to be a comedy, with Elvis as a rodeo-riding, womanizing Navajo Indian. The sketchy storyline involves Elvis being threatened with jail by the American government for selling cows that are not his property. *Speedway*, released in the summer of 1968, was a milestone in that it marked the last soundtrack LP from a Presley movie. Elvis stars as stock-car racing driver Steve Grayson, who is investigated by tax inspector(!) Nancy Sinatra. His financial affairs are complicated by his generosity and his manager's gambling debts, but Nancy, who is impressed by Elvis's singing (and even duets with him), eventually

succumbs to his charms, and helps him resolve his financial problems.

Having begun the decade on an astonishing wave of popularity with enormous hits like *It's Now Or Never* (which eventually sold over nine million copies world-wide), *Are You Lonesome Tonight*, *Surrender*, *Good Luck Charm* and *Return To Sender*, all of which had topped the charts on both sides of the Atlantic, by 1968 his records were struggling to reach even the bottom of the chart. *Speedway*, as well as being the final soundtrack LP was also the lowest placed of his albums during the 1960s, rising only to Number 82.

The decline had begun in 1963, and had grown more evident during the following

Above: 'These boots were made for jiving.' With Nancy Sinatra in 'Speedway'.

Opposite top: With the Wiere Brothers in 'Double Trouble'.

Opposite bottom: Entertaining in 'Clambake'.

111

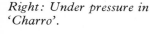

Above: Elvis as snapper in 'Live A Little, Love A Little'. The model is Michelle Carey.

Right: Under pressure in 'Charro'.

when Elvis was back at RCA's Nashville studio working on material that would not be sacrificed in films, with a new record producer, Felton Jarvis, who introduced new songwriters like Jerry Reed, in 1967. An even more important boost to his flagging career came with a T.V. Special recorded in June, 1968, and screened a few months later, just before Christmas, and this rebirth will be discussed in the next chapter.

As already mentioned, Elvis still had film commitments, which resulted in four more movies, the last of which was made in 1970. 'Live A Little, Love A Little' was released in late 1968, and featured Elvis as a Los Angeles photographer who develops a curious relationship with a girl played by Michele Carey. They meet on a beach, where he is seeking isolation while she wants company, and he is forced to stay in the sea for several hours by Michele's overgrown Great Dane, Albert, catching pneumonia as a result. Despite feeling upset and confused, Elvis managed by the end of the film to fall in love with Michele, and has time to sing four songs, two of which *A Little More Conversation* and *Almost In Love*, were released as a single that managed a mere four weeks near the foot of the chart.

The first of two 1969 films, 'Charro',

two years – the Danish authors of the book 'Elvis – Recording Sessions' summed up the situation neatly with the statement 'What happened in '64–'66 is best described as an attempt at artistic suicide'. It seems unlikely that any other artist could have survived after recording so many poor songs or appearing in such weak films, but Elvis had such a special talent and strong appeal that he was able to rise again. The improvements had actually begun during the woeful film period,

A still from 'Charro', in which Elvis played a very different role from most of his 1960s films.

A still from 'Change Of Habit', which co-starred Mary Tyler Moore as a nun.

Elvis experiencing 'The Trouble With Girls' with co-star Marlyn Mason, and (opposite) receiving an award on the set of 'The Trouble With Girls', earned by his British Fan Club, who had raised funds to provide guide dogs for the blind.

marked a return to straight acting for Elvis for the first time since the relatively unsuccessful 'Flaming Star' in 1961. Wearing a beard (for the first and only time in a movie), Elvis plays a former outlaw who is trying to forsake his wicked ways but is framed by his old gang. When his freind the sheriff is shot, Elvis takes over as a lawman, and defeats the bad guys after a battle, before setting off for Mexico and a new life. The only song featured was *Charro*, performed over the credits.

The other 1969 movie, 'The Trouble With Girls (And How To Get Into It)', included only three songs, and was set in the Roaring Twenties, with Elvis as the manager of a travelling show known as the Chautauqua. Arriving in the town of Radford Center, he encounters a variety of problems with his performers and the local townsfolk, and a murder mystery occurs, which he solves, of course.

The last of these films, 'Change Of Habit', saw Elvis in a serious role as a doctor working in a ghetto area. He is temporarily assisted by a trio of nuns (although he is unaware of their calling as they wear normal clothes), one of whom is Mary Tyler Moore. Elvis and Mary fall in love, at which point she is forced to make the agonizing choice between God and Elvis. 'Could he change her life? Could she forget her vows and follow her heart?' asked the posters outside every cinema, but the answer was not provided in the film. While he would go on to largely retrieve his screen appeal with two acclaimed documentaries later in the 1970s, Presley's acting career ended with audiences having to decide whether they knew (or even cared) what was going to happen next.

THE GREATEST ENTERTAINER IN THE WORLD

Below: Elvis's guitar (fourth from right) on show at Expo '67 in Canada.

After the retrogressive years of the mid-1960s when his career had plumbed the depths with a succession of mediocre films and uninspired soundtrack albums, Elvis was back at the top by 1970, living up to a new name which Colonel Parker had conceived for him – 'The Greatest Entertainer In The World'. Just as the Sixties had begun with Elvis on the crest of a new wave of popularity, so did the Seventies – loved by fans and acclaimed by music critics, Presley's albums and singles regained their almost permanent position in the Top Ten of the world's charts, while his live shows at Las Vegas, which were his first public appearances in nearly a decade, broke box office records. This revitalization was not something that occurred overnight, and its beginnings can be traced back as far as 1966, perhaps the least credible year of Elvis's career thus far, and a studio session that occurred during the latter part of May during that year. Although few fans recognized it at

the time, this was the turning point, and the upward swing became obvious as a result of a television show transmitted during December 1968, and a highly productive period of recording in Memphis, Tennessee, a few weeks later.

The 1966 sessions emerged on record in the shape of a gospel album, *How Great Thou Art*, which is generally considered to be the most successful Elvis album of his cinematic period. In retrospect, it no longer seems particularly remarkable, but it certainly stood head and shoulders above his film soundtrack albums of the time, won a Grammy award for the best gospel performance of the year, and was incidentally certified gold. The most significant aspect of the recording sessions was that a different record producer, Felton Jarvis, had been assigned to work with Elvis, replacing Chet Atkins who had decided that it was time to stand down after overseeing Presley's career for RCA for a decade. Atkins' methods had never been very forceful when he was working with Elvis, since the latter was largely in control as regards selecting material and working out arrangements with his accompanying musicians – many critics felt that Atkins could and should have exerted the influence of his position more forcibly, especially in changing the musical direction of Elvis's records away from the drift into increasingly familiar sounding songs.

Felton Jarvis was a good choice as the catalyst to reawaken Presley's flagging career – first and foremost, he was an Elvis fan and, in 1959, had actually cut a tribute record, *Don't Knock Elvis*, for the Viva label. After this he had worked as a producer for ABC/Dot Records, with such artists as Tommy Roe, Fats Domino, Lloyd Price and even Gladys Knight and

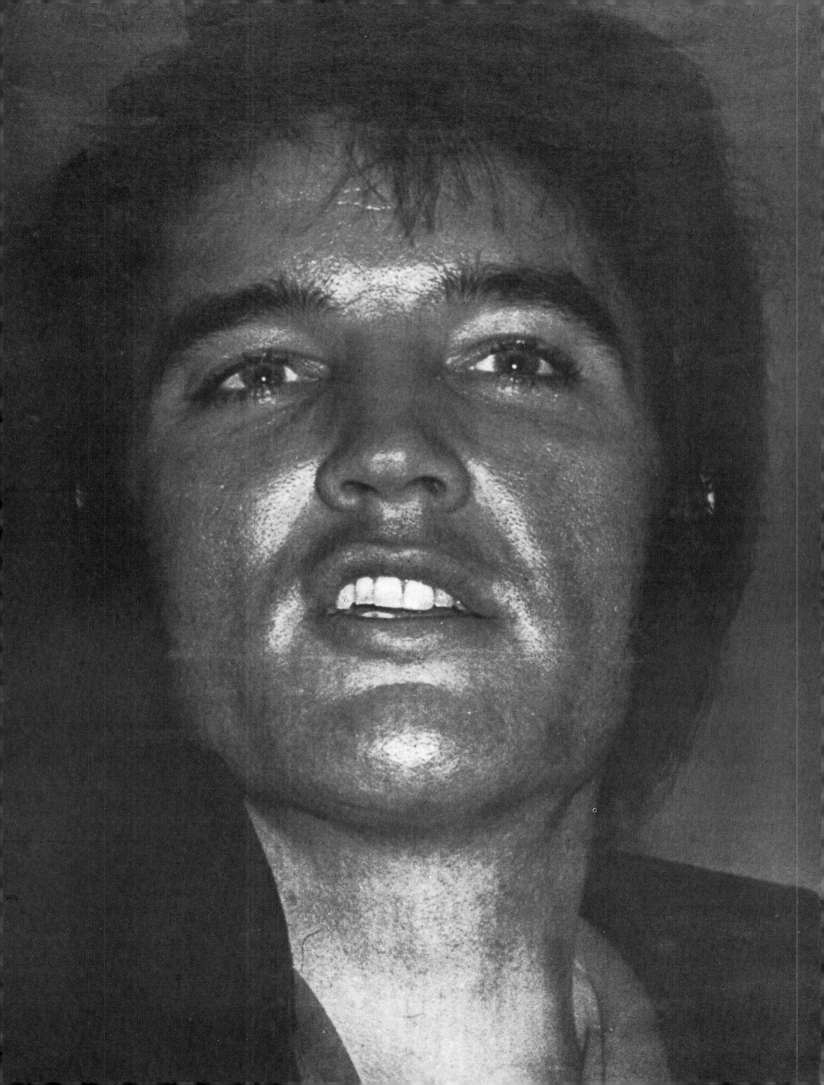

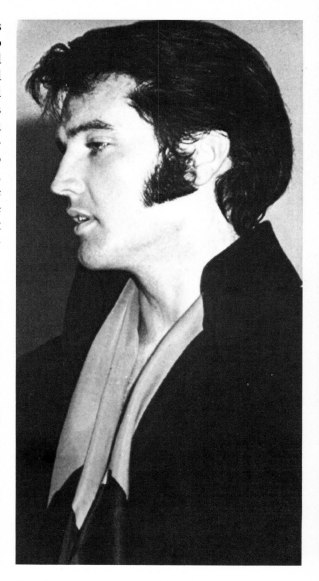

Right: Elvis at the 1969 press conference announcing his Las Vegas concerts, and (opposite) Priscilla and Elvis after their Las Vegas wedding.

the Pips, before moving to RCA. Jarvis realized that major changes would have to be made if Elvis were to survive and prosper as a popular entertainer, and while he could do little with the material already selected for film projects, he was able to influence the choice of songs from demo recordings sent to Elvis for non-soundtrack sessions, and could also introduce some different musicians, although any changes of this nature were of minor importance compared to the need for improved material that might improve Elvis's image with the record-buying public.

Teenage fans of the Beatles and other popular Sixties' acts held Elvis in very low regard, leaving their older brothers and sisters, and in some cases, even their parents, to buy Presley records. The main problem was that the Hill and Range publishing system, which supplied Elvis with all his material, was now outdated and old-fashioned. With some notable exceptions, like *Viva Las Vegas* and *Devil In Disguise*, both composed by Doc Pomus and Mort Shuman, the songs that Freddie Bienstock was supplying on demo records seemed more often than not to be dull and uninspired retreads of earlier hits. Almost all the best songwriters of the late 1950s and early 1960s, including Jerry Leiber and Mike Stoller, had stopped sending material to Hill and Range, while the best-selling composers who had subsequently come to the fore were either performers, like Bob Dylan, John Lennon and Paul McCartney, or worked for specialist rock publishers as opposed to show business companies like Hill and Range. However, Jarvis gradually began to introduce Elvis to new songs and new writers, including Jerry Reed, a talented guitarist based in Nashville, who later found fame both as a country-music star and in films.

In September 1967, Presley cut Reed's *Guitar Man*, and during the following January, *U.S. Male*, another Reed composition, and in both cases Reed himself participated in the sessions and provided some quicksilver guitar work, with the result that these tracks were among the best released by Elvis in the second half of the 1960s, and both became sizeable hits during 1968, although with higher chart positions in Britain than America. Felton

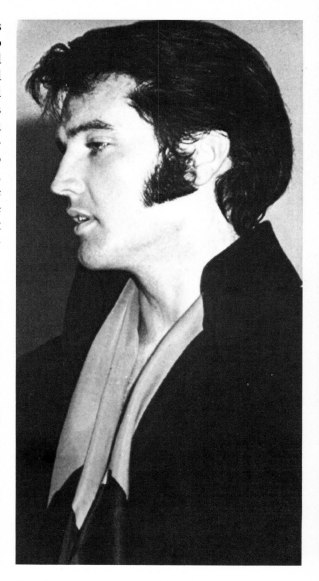

Jarvis also persuaded Presley to return to recording rock'n'roll songs from the previous decade, including Tommy Tucker's *Hi-Heel Sneakers*, Jimmy Reed's bluesy *Big Boss Man* and Chuck Berry's *Too Much Monkey Business*.

The Nashville sessions co-ordinated by Jarvis featured Scotty Moore, D.J. Fontana, Floyd Cramer and several others who had played on Elvis's records for years, but also introduced some younger musicians who went on to make considerable reputations for themselves in the 1970s, like Charlie McCoy, who became the best-known harmonica man in Nashville, guitarist Chip Young, who later emerged as a highly rated producer of country music, trumpeter Ray Stevens, who developed into a best-selling country/pop singer and writer, and pianist David Briggs. With new songs, fresh writers and bright young musicians, Felton Jarvis helped Elvis to return to his best form, although it took a little while before the public were convinced of the improvement, as the majority of radio-station programmers responsible for selecting the records that made up the all-important play lists had virtually given up listening to new Presley releases assuming reasonably enough, that they would all sound much the same.

The first major change in Elvis of which the public became aware had nothing to do with music. His relinquishment of bachelorhood, when he married Priscilla at the start of May 1967, no doubt broke numerous female hearts. More significantly, it was the first real news about Elvis since his discharge from the Army seven years before.

Priscilla Beaulieu was now twenty-one (Elvis was thirty-two) and had been living at Graceland for six years. Her parents had become increasingly concerned because the marriage which Elvis had promised would take place showed no signs of happening. Many of his associates felt that it was unlikely that their boss would ever marry, as he seemed so set in his bachelor ways and it was no secret that he was in the habit of dating other girls while he was in California. However, Elvis did want to get married, and had apparently been keen to do so even before 1967. Gabe Tucker, an ex-employee of Colonel Parker, explained in the book 'Up and Down With Elvis Presley' that Elvis had first suggested getting married when his movie career was at its peak, but that Parker had asked him to postpone his plans: 'The Colonel was asking that Elvis save the announcement for months or years, until a time when his career needed pumping up,' reported Tucker, 'And months later, when the Colonel felt Elvis needed a press hype, he told Elvis "Now would be a wonderful time for you and Priscilla to marry".'

The Colonel took over the planning of the wedding and, typically, set about gaining the maximum publicity – rather than making an official announcement he shrouded everything in secrecy and then dropped hints to reporters. On April 30, Parker's business associates at the various film companies, at RCA and at the William Morris Agency, received mysterious telegrams instructing them to fly to Las Vegas, which was puzzling since

both the newspapers and the airwaves were carrying news that Elvis and Priscilla were holidaying at Palm Springs, where it was rumoured that they would plight their troth. In the early hours of May 1, Elvis and his bride-to-be flew to Las Vegas aboard a private Lear Jet and at 3.00 a.m., visited the Clark County courthouse where they spent $15 on a marriage licence, which might be considered unusual behaviour anywhere else in the world but in Vegas, where 'instant' marriages are commonplace, and everything including County courthouses, apes the Windmill theatre in never closing.

The couple then drove to the Aladdin Hotel, which was owned by Colonel Parker's good friend Milton Prell. Parker's associates were also staying at the hotel, but still had no idea what was going to happen even when they found the lobby full of reporters that morning. Stan Brossette of M.G.M. recalled: 'We had breakfast and then returned to our rooms, and were told to call no one. Shortly after that, he finally told us, but I still don't know why the mystery – it was just something the Colonel did.'

The ceremony had been organized by a member of Elvis's entourage, Marty Lacker, although he was in the dark about some of the arrangements, and a few hours before the event was due to occur, he discovered that most of the groom's friends had not been invited either to the wedding or to the reception, which shocked him. In his book, 'Elvis: Portrait Of A Friend', Lacker reports 'The reason given was that there wouldn't be enough room in the suite where the ceremony would be held, but as it turned out, there was plenty of room. I don't know who made the decision, but I don't believe it was Elvis. It was a bad decision'.

Elvis and Priscilla were married at approximately 9.40 a.m. by Judge David Zenoff, a justice of the Nevada Supreme Court, in Milton Prell's private suite at the Aladdin. The simple ceremony lasted just eight minutes, and Elvis wore a stylish black tuxedo, which had been designed by Marty Lacker, while Priscilla wore a white chiffon gown with a six-foot train. She promised to love, honour, cherish and comfort (but not obey) Elvis, and her ring was breathtaking and had obviously cost a small fortune – a three-carat diamond surrounded by a cluster of twenty smaller diamonds. There were only eleven guests: Vernon and Dee Presley, Major and Mrs. Beaulieu, Colonel and Mrs. Parker, George Klein (a schoolfriend of Elvis), Marty Lacker and Joe Esposito (who were joint best man and the only members of the groom's entourage present), Joe's wife, Joan, who was matron of honour, and the bride's sister, Michelle, who was maid of honour.

After the wedding, there was a brief press conference for the reporters, who were still recovering from a night spent rushing from their offices to Palm Springs, and from there to Las Vegas. Revelations during the press conference were few – Elvis admitted, 'Ed Sullivan didn't scare me this much!', but several pressmen were surprised to learn that he had known Priscilla since the Army days, and Elvis explained: 'Priscilla was one of the few girls who was interested in me, for me alone. We never discussed marriage in Germany – we just met at her father's house, went to the movies, and did a lot of driving – that's all. I waited for her to grow up. We shall continue to live in Memphis, and we hope to spend a lot of time on my new horse farm in Mississippi'. After talking to the press, Elvis joined Priscilla and their respective families for the wedding breakfast, a sumptuous spread with roast sucking pig, ham and eggs, fried chicken, clam oysters,

Equestrian Elvis, 1968, and (below) Elvis on his horse Rising Sun at Graceland.

champagne and a five-foot-high wedding cake.

Colonel Parker regarded the wedding he'd stage-managed as a great success – he had achieved maximum publicity for his 'boy' at a time when Elvis's career was in need of a boost, he had avoided problems with crowds of fans because the speed with which the ceremony had taken place meant that they were unaware of it until it was over and, more to the point, perhaps, he had also managed to persuade his wealthy friend, the hotel proprietor, to pay for almost everything.

The newly weds flew back to Palm Springs, where they had left the bemused Presley entourage – Marty Lacker reported, 'Most of the guys left for Los Angeles, and they were as mad as hell!' Elvis himself flew to California after a couple of days spent putting the finishing touches to the 'Clambake' movie, following which he rejoined Priscilla, and the couple flew to the Bahamas for their honeymoon, although it seems that Elvis failed to enjoy it as much as he might have, as he found the islands disappointing. Europe was his original idea for a honeymoon location, and he and Priscilla had gone as far as acquiring new passports, but the Colonel vetoed that plan because the ever-interested European promoters had been told that Presley's commitments were so heavy that there was no chance of fitting in a tour, or even a visit, to Europe. Elvis may have complained about the Colonel to his friends, but he continued to follow his manager's advice and suggestions even when they related to personal matters.

Elvis and Priscilla went from the honeymoon to the Mississippi ranch mentioned at the press conference. Earlier in the year Elvis had been out on his motorcycle with his friends in tow. Their ride had taken them some distance to the south of Memphis and across the Tenn-

Priscilla on horseback.

essee state line. They had come upon a ranch at Walls, Mississippi, which Elvis had immediately decided to buy – Priscilla loved horse riding and Elvis thought it would make the perfect place for their home. After paying $30,000 for the 163-acre 'Circle G' property (soon to be renamed 'Flying Circle G', since there was already a 'Circle G' in Texas) in February, he began spending hundreds of thousands of dollars on pick-up trucks, mobile homes for his entourage and extensive alterations, including the rebuilding of the walls to deter intruders, plus stocking the stables with prize-winning horses, while Alan Fortas was the Presley aide placed in charge of the ranch.

This expenditure on the ranch was by no means the sum total of Elvis's outlay during 1967 on property and development. Six days after his wedding, he purchased 1174 Hillcrest Road, a luxurious home in Beverly Hills, California for $400,000. High on a hill, the multi-level home, with a huge swimming pool, had a spectacular view over Los Angeles. Elvis went on a massive spending spree, redecorating, remodelling and adding a recreation room. Additionally, he was frequently ordering extensions, improvements and alterations at Graceland, where the furnishings changed every few months. While he was apparently miserly

in his payment of wages, Elvis was very generous to his employees in other ways, often giving them lavish presents. Beside the entourage, which normally averaged around a dozen, there was an additional staff of ten people at Gracelands, including two secretaries, maids, cooks, two gardeners, three gatemen (one of whom was Elvis's Uncle Vester), and even Vernon Presley, who was on the Graceland payroll, his main task being to supervise the payment of bills.

Vernon was shocked by the huge sums his son was spending, and soon realized

Elvis's Uncle Vester on duty as gate guard at Graceland.

that despite the colossal income from movies, records and music publishing, Elvis was managing to spend nearly all of it, and after trying, without success, to put a brake on Elvis's spending, he asked the Colonel to help. Parker used Elvis's marriage as one excuse to order some cuts in the size of the entourage, decreeing that some of the paid companions would now be unnecessary as Elvis had Priscilla – in his book 'The Truth About Elvis', Larry Geller remembers Parker telling the men 'Things are going to change around here – Elvis has been spending too much money lately, and has gone beyond what he can afford'. Even so, Elvis never found it easy to restrict his spending, and over the years would become more and more generous, although he did realize the folly of purchasing the Flying Circle G, which he rarely had time to visit. In 1969, the ranch was sold, after which the Presleys divided their time between homes in Memphis and California.

To pay for his homes and expensive life-style – he also spent vast amounts on cars, jewels and guns – Elvis had to keep earning more and more money, and as the film income began to decrease, Colonel Parker started to look for other, more lucrative, projects and in January 1968, he was able to announce that Presley would be appearing on a T.V. Special for NBC, sponsored by Singer Sewing Machines, for which Elvis would receive $500,000, an enormous sum, even for one of his stature in the show business world.

A month later came the news that Elvis had become a father, when Priscilla gave birth to a 6 lb 15 oz daughter, Lisa Marie Presley, at 5.01 p.m. on February 1, 1968, in a room on the fifth floor of the Baptist Memorial Hospital in Memphis. It had been nine months to the day since the wedding in Las Vegas.

Colonel Parker's concept for the upcoming T.V. Special was 'Elvis And The Wonderful World Of Christmas', but the show's director, Steve Binder, had very different plans. He possessed strong opinions about the way rock music should be presented on television, and had been partially responsible for a T.V. film, 'The T.A.M.I. Show', a few years before, which had featured often breathtakingly exciting live footage of acts like James Brown, the Ronettes, the Supremes and the Rolling Stones. Binder said: 'I felt very, very strongly that the T.V. Special was Elvis's moment of truth, because if he treated the Special like another M.G.M. movie, he would wipe out his career and would only be known as the phenomenon who came along in the Fifties, shook his hips and had a great manager. On the reverse side, if he could do a Special and prove that he was still Number One, he could have a whole rejuvenation thing going'.

Binder succeeded in separating Elvis from the Colonel's influence for long enough to convince Presley that the

Right: Priscilla leaves hospital with Lisa Marie Presley and the proud father, and (far right) Elvis and Lisa Marie at Graceland in 1968.

Opposite: One of the first family photographs after Lisa Marie's birth.

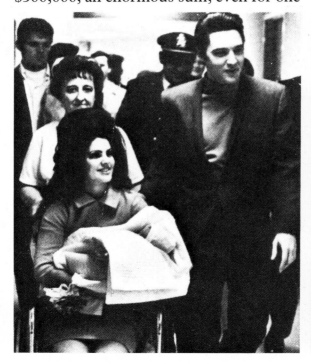

Christmas idea was hardly an inspired notion, but he had a continual battle with Parker over songs and sets. The Colonel, as usual, was being ultra-shrewd – he didn't try to prevent Elvis from breaking new ground, but he exaggerated his objections to ensure that Binder was kept on his toes at all times, and as a result, the director committed himself completely to the project, supported by NBC, who provided a huge budget for the fabulous sets and the large supporting cast of musicians and dancers. Elvis and Steve Binder got on famously, and before long, the star was contributing his own ideas to the Special – between rehearsals he would tell jokes and stories about his early days in the music business, and some of them, carefully scripted to resemble off-the-cuff remarks, were used in the final show.

As part of his efforts to key Elvis up for his performance, Binder argued that if Presley were to walk about on a public street, no one would recognize him. Elvis, having spent more than a decade away from the outside world because he was unable to appear in public without being mobbed, didn't believe that Binder's assertion could be true, but agreed to test the theory by going from Binder's office onto Sunset Strip. There, he was virtually ignored by everyone for fifteen minutes, or at least not openly recognized – Sunset Strip in 1968 was one of the 'hippest' thoroughfares in the world, and perhaps it would have been ultimately 'uncool' to notice someone as apparently passé as Elvis. Whatever the reason for his anonymity, that quarter of an hour had a profound effect on Elvis – although he had frequently felt frustrated at his inability to lead a normal life because of his over-enthusiastic fan following, the fact that people no longer recognized him dented his pride, and like everyone else associated with the T.V. Special, he became determined to give of his best, going on a strict diet to lose weight, practising his 'ad lib' lines and rehearsing the choreographed routines. None of his films, with the possible exception of the very earliest movies ten years before, had ever been taken so seriously by their star.

The show was simply called 'Elvis', and combined segments from two live shows, taped before invited audiences at the NBC Studios in Hollywood, with some

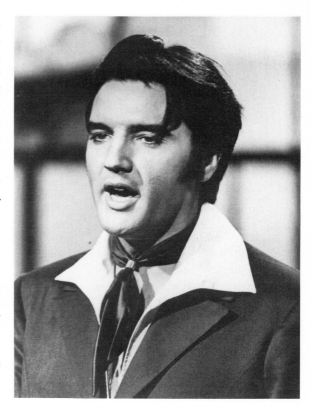

elaborate set pieces in which he mimed to pre-recorded tracks. The live portions involved Elvis sitting on a stage shaped like, and no bigger than, a boxing ring, surrounded on all four sides by avid fans. He wore a black leather suit with a high collar, specially designed by Bill Belew, who would later design his Las Vegas stage costumes, and he had grown his sideburns again. He was backed by a handful of musicians and friends, including Scotty Moore, D.J. Fontana and Charlie Hodge, with whom he chatted and joked and performed songs from the 1950s. Elvis, who had not appeared before a live audience since the Pearl Harbour shows in 1961, was exceptionally nervous at the start, making numerous mistakes, but the sections selected to be shown on television captured him at his very best – he had rarely looked and sounded so good. The set pieces involved musical support from an orchestra augmented by several of the Los Angeles session musicians who had contributed to the film soundtracks, including drummer Hal Blaine, Larry Knechtel on bass and Don Randi on piano, while the performance of *Guitar Man* involved thirty-five dancers and a similar number of musicians. More production numbers were shot than were needed – one scene, set in a bordello, was dropped because both the Colonel and the

NBC hierarchy judged it unsuitable for a family audience, although Steve Binder later commented, 'It happens to have been the best scene for which I've ever been responsible'. One solitary seasonal song, *Blue Christmas*, was salvaged by Colonel Tom Parker from his original concept.

Binder wanted the show to conclude with Elvis performing a song with a 'message', and despite very strong objections from the Colonel, who was reluctant to have Elvis involved with lyrics that might appear to be controversial, the director was able to convince Elvis that it was a good idea. Songwriter Earl Brown was commissioned to write a song which showed that 'Elvis cares', and overnight came up with *If I Can Dream*. While the lyrics of the song could hardly be termed controversial in any way, Elvis gave a dramatic and very powerful performance, which was a perfect end to the show. When it was released as a single, *If I Can Dream* became his biggest American hit since 1965.

The T.V. Special was a great success — recorded during the summer of 1968, it was screened in America on December 3, and captured the night's top ratings. In Britain it was screened on New Year's Eve. The soundtrack LP *Elvis – TV Special*, reached the Top Ten in America,

A composite of Elvis shot in 1969.

were recorded in Las Vegas, at a series of fifty-seven shows performed by Elvis at the International Hotel in August.

This return to live work was the high point of 1969 – Colonel Parker chose Las Vegas as the place to relaunch Elvis's career as a performer for several reasons, largely financial. He had originally considered a series of shows at large stadia around the United States, but the money offered by the brand new International Hotel – one million dollars for a month-long season – was better than he could have obtained anywhere else. Las Vegas was a holiday resort that attracted visitors from all over the world, and although appearing there was far from being a solution to the international demand for Elvis, it did represent a token gesture to foreign fans, albeit the more opulent among them. Parker also liked Las Vegas because gambling was one of his leisure activities and he was well cared for by the local hotel and casino operators.

Elvis might have been sceptical about playing Las Vegas after his unhappy experience at the Frontier Hotel in 1956, when his shows had been so poorly received that the Colonel had been forced to cancel the second week of his booking, but in 1968, he and Priscilla had seen Tom Jones appearing at the Flamingo Hotel, and the evening had convinced him that Las Vegas was quite definitely the best place to re-embark upon live performances. Jones, a Welsh singer, regarded Elvis as his major influence, and Elvis in return was very friendly to Jones, and once said 'Tom is the only man who has ever come anywhere close to the way I sing'. He watched Jones's very professional show with great interest, and was amazed at the screams and near-hysterical behaviour the Welshman elicited from the middle-aged ladies in the audience, especially when he wiped his brow with a handkerchief which he then threw into the auditorium for his eager fans to fight over.

The response reminded Elvis of the reactions of the teenage girls among his own following during the 1950s, and backstage after the show, Jones talked to Elvis about performing in Las Vegas. They discussed the best way to handle audiences and the type of songs which were most popular – Elvis was very attracted by the Vegas style, particularly the lavish costumes and stage sets, the close communication with the audience and the full sound of the hotel orchestras, and decided that his shows would be as lavish and spectacular as possible, with the emphasis on quality, saying: 'I don't care if I don't make any money, as long as I give them a good show.'

He had no intention of trying to repeat the live portions of the 1968 T.V. Special with the small band, old hits, Fifties-style leather jacket and sideburns. His Las Vegas revue would introduce a 'new style' Elvis Presley, offering professional entertainment for an adult audience, pursuant to which he set about hiring the best available musicians, plus both male and

The glittering 'Strip' of Las Vegas, Nevada.

female vocal groups, planned his routine with some appropriate between-songs patter, and asked designer Bill Belew to devise a comfortable but impressive stage costume.

It was clear that Elvis was taking this new venture very seriously when he flew to Los Angeles for two weeks of rehearsal with the band, who were indeed among the best musicians money could buy: leader and guitarist James Burton had made his name as Ricky Nelson's right-hand man, and could rarely be tempted out of the studios as he made so much money from session work. He claims to have turned down the chance to work with Bob Dylan because he would have lost too much money, and perhaps more to the point, might have lost his position as the number one session guitarist in Los Angeles if he were unavailable for an extended period. The rest of the band, which Burton selected, included Jerry Scheff on bass, Ronnie Tutt on drums, Larry Muhoberac on keyboards and vocalist guitarist John Wilkinson. Elvis's aide Charlie Hodge was also a vital element of the band, playing acoustic guitar and handling backing vocals, although his main function was to act as intermediary between the musicians and Elvis (his other job was to supply Elvis with towels, the thirst-quenching Gatorade drink, and anything else he might require). They prepared over 100 songs, mixing Elvis's best-known hits with several of his most recent recordings and a number of hit songs primarily associated with other artists.

Elvis went to Las Vegas two weeks before his season started to check out the facilities at the hotel, to watch and meet Barbra Streisand, the singer who had opened the spectacular Showroom Internationale on July 2, to rehearse with his male and female vocal groups, the Imperials and the Sweet Inspirations respectively, and the hotel's twenty-five piece orchestra led by Bobby Morris. He also wanted to practice his choreographed routines, which incorporated the kicks and movements used in his favourite sport, karate – Bill Belew's ingenious one-piece stage costume was based on a karate suit.

The International was the biggest and most opulent hotel in Las Vegas, having been constructed at a cost over $60 million. It stood thirty storeys high, had 1519 rooms, and its swimming pool was the second largest body of water in the state of Nevada (after Lake Mead). Barbra Streisand had been contracted to open the hotel's main showroom (with a seating capacity of around 2000 people), on the assumption that she was the biggest contemporary attraction in the United States, having recently won an Oscar for Best Actress for her role in the musical film, 'Funny Girl'. While her shows did excellent business, they were less than sell-outs, unlike Elvis's appearances, which seemed set to break all manner of box-office records. As soon as Ms. Streisand's season came to an end, Colonel Parker organized the plastering of every available space with posters proclaiming Elvis 'The World's Greatest Entertainer', and at a press conference, the singer admitted that he was nervous, but was nevertheless glad to be back performing for real audiences, explaining 'I chose Las Vegas because it's a place people come to from all over'. When asked whether he felt it had been a mistake to release so many soundtrack albums, Elvis admitted that he certainly thought so.

A huge press contingent was in attendance for the opening night, all of them invited by the hotel management which went so far as to also pay for the critics' transportation, while the invitation-only audience also included Sam Phillips, Fifties singing stars Fats Domino and Pat Boone, folk singer Phil Ochs and orchestra leader Henry Mancini. What this crowd watched on July 26, 1969, the occasion of Elvis's debut Las Vegas performance, set the tone and style for the many shows he would subsequently give in the resort city during the 1970s – the adapted karate costume and movements to match, the top-notch musical support, the heavenly voices of the backing singers, the frequent ad-libbing and monologues between songs, and the close contact with the audience, and in particular the female contingent. He sang medleys of old hits, current successes like *Suspicious Minds*, due for imminent release as a single, and hits associated with others, like Paul McCartney's *Yesterday*, and won a deserved standing ovation and high praise from the assembled journalists – the prestigious magazine 'Newsweek' noted: 'There are several unbelievable things about Elvis, but the most incredible is his staying power in a world where meteoric careers fade like shooting stars'. The second night found Elvis more relaxed now that the pressure of being scrutinized by critics had largely abated, and he began to establish even greater rapport with the audience, utilizing the handkerchief and scarf techniques he had picked up from Tom Jones, which won a reaction similar to that which Jones had received, with screams and near hysteria, and initiated a ritual between Elvis and his adoring female fans that would continue for several years.

His season at the International Hotel ran for a month, with two shows each night, and every performance was a total sell-out, which delighted the hotel management, as Presley's presence boosted takings at all their facilities, including the gaming tables and the one-armed bandit slot machines, with the result that Elvis was rebooked for a further month-long engagement in January 1970, which some observers considered was too soon after the triumphant debut. Evidently they were wrong, as once again the demand for tickets far exceeded the

The 1969 Las Vegas season. Above: Elvis meets rock writer/disc jockey Rodney Bingenheimer and British rock legend Screaming Lord Sutch.

Elvis and Priscilla flanked by Vernon Presley (far right).

Elvis with two adoring fans.

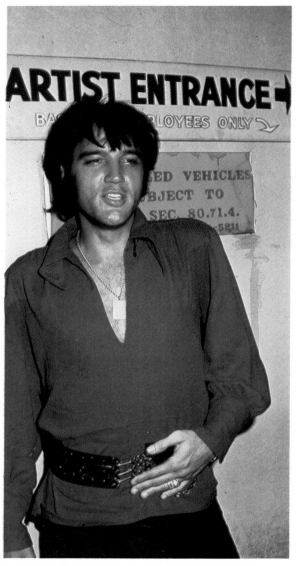

Above: Elvis besieged by autograph hunters, 1970, and (right) a welcome breath of backstage air.

supply. After his month in Vegas, Elvis was happy but exhausted, and he adjourned to Palm Springs for a holiday with Priscilla, before travelling to Nashville to re-record some vocals for the upcoming 'Vegas/Memphis' live album, after which he returned to Memphis to relax, prepare for the next shows, and celebrate the festive season.

1970 dawned with Elvis at the very top of the entertainment world – he would have certainly been recognized on Sunset Strip at this point, and the combination of the T.V. Special, the Memphis recordings and the live Las Vegas shows meant that he was the most popular performer anywhere. He was at a peak from which, sadly, he could only descend.

For the second Las Vegas season, there were a few changes in the musical line up – Glen D. Hardin (a long-time member of the post-Buddy Holly Crickets) was introduced as pianist and also apparently assisted James Burton in leading the band, while J.D. Sumner and the Stamps replaced the Imperials as the male backing vocal group, and Kathy Westmoreland, who was to become a staple of Elvis's Las Vegas shows, made her first appearance. Charlie Hodge was retained as the star's right-hand man, as Elvis liked to change the running order of his show each night, and Hodge compiled the list of songs. Among other changes, Elvis's costume was even more jewel-bedecked, while his repertoire included more contemporary pop standards, including Del Shannon's *Runaway*, the Bee Gees' *Words*, and *Hey Jude* by the Beatles.

Presley's female fans, some of whom had bought his earliest records when they were still teenagers during the 1950s, were becoming increasingly uninhibited, and it became quite usual for room keys to be thrown onstage during his act (and for sheepish husbands to retrieve them afterwards). Some women even jumped on stage and tried to hug and kiss the object of their lust, but most were intercepted and returned, gently but firmly, to their seats. They could be dangerous, as Red West, one of the Presley aides responsible for security, explained: 'Elvis was caught more than once by an accidental punch in the eye, or a long finger nail raking across his cheek. His fans didn't mean to hurt him, but they did, and they would have

pulled him to pieces if he didn't have protection.'

In February 1970, Elvis travelled to Houston, Texas, for shows at the Astrodome, the world's largest covered stadium, which was an excellent venue for baseball and rodeo events, but proved most unsatisfactory for concerts, as the sound echoed around the vast arena. The shows had seemed like a good idea – Elvis had been very keen to play for his fans who had been so supportive during the early days, and the Colonel had been guaranteed $100,000 for each concert – but

subsequent shows outside Las Vegas took place in concert halls or smaller sports facilities. In August, he returned to the International Hotel in Las Vegas for a third month-long season, and the hotel announced his presence with the single word 'Elvis' in huge letters above its entrance. The 'Elvis Summer Festival', as it was billed, was also the point at which his first meaningful film of the 1970s was shot – a documentary titled 'Elvis – That's The Way It Is', which was directed by Denis Sanders. A film crew followed Elvis during preparations for the show,

Performing in Las Vegas – a still from the film documentary 'Elvis – That's The Way It Is', 1970.

135

and several fans were filmed, including one couple, Bob and Nancy Neal, who had met while attending a previous Elvis concert and decided to marry while their hero was in Las Vegas, although the majority of the movie concentrated on Elvis's show, and featured performance's of twenty-seven songs. If you were in town when Elvis was performing, it was impossible to ignore him, as he was advertised constantly on the radio (an unnecessary extravagance, as all his shows were sold out, but one which suited the Colonel's belief in maximum publicity), while anyone staying at the International Hotel received a catalogue of Elvis's RCA recordings whenever they ordered anything from room service!

During September, Elvis went on tour, visiting several major American cities including St. Louis, Detroit and Phoenix, and after a month's break was back on the road this time performing on the West Coast and in Oklahoma and Colorado. On these tours, an entire floor of each selected hotel was requisitioned by Presley's staff, and security was so tight that no outsider

could get close to him. It was during this period that Elvis became increasingly nocturnal in his habits. Foil was stuck over windows to allow him to sleep during the daylight hours, and Presley aide Jerry Schilling told Jerry Hopkins: 'We lived long hours, slept in the daytime and started to take sleeping pills to make it easy, but after a while, one wasn't enough. Sometimes, for a weight problem or to wake up for an early studio call, we'd take a diet pill, and over a period of time, one diet pill wasn't enough . . .'. While the tours were certainly exhausting, his habitual use of pills eventually began to have an extremely debilitating effect on Elvis, and it became clear that the stresses and strains of touring were far greater than film making had been.

In January 1971, Elvis was back in Las Vegas, by which time the International Hotel had been renamed the Hilton, and it was during this season that a death threat was made against Elvis, which was taken very seriously by both the Presley entourage and the F.B.I., although no attempt on his life was actually made, nor

were any suspects arrested. Several members of the Presley clan were special deputies for the Memphis Police Department, this status having been granted to allow them to carry automatic weapons, which were illegal for normal citizens, to help them with their security duties at Presley shows.

Elvis had received his first death threat during the early 1960s, and at the time, an F.B.I. man had advised the singer to arm himself, as a result of which he had carried a gun ever since, usually a small pistol which he kept in his boot or under his belt, and wore even when he was on stage in Las Vegas. He loved collecting police badges and guns of all kinds – according to Becky Yancey, a secretary at Graceland for many years, 'He was enchanted with law enforcement, and gave presents of expensive new cars to policemen. He told me that, as a teenager, he had wanted to be a policeman', and Presley aide Marty Lacker reported: 'Elvis helped a lot of police departments with their youth programmes, particularly in Memphis. For years, he was

137

Right: Elvis onstage in 1970.

Opposite top: Elvis caught unawares in 1971.

Opposite bottom: A famous meeting at the White House, the Presidential Residence in Washington, D.C., in late 1970 between then President Richard Nixon and the King of Rock'n'Roll.

intensely interested in the work that police and sheriff's departments were doing with young people'. From time to time, Elvis would visit the Memphis Police Department, and even practised shooting at their firing range.

Late in 1970, Elvis became obsessed with the idea of working for the Federal Narcotics Bureau – he knew that many rock performers habitually took hard drugs like cocaine and heroin (which he curiously rationalized as completely different from the sleeping pills and diet 'medication' that he ingested), and thought that if he had an official Narcotics badge, he might be able to influence them into changing their habits. This was without doubt a very bizarre notion, but Elvis was determined to carry it through, and in December, he travelled to Washington to offer his services to the Deputy Director of the Federal Narcotics Bureau. When the request was predictably denied, Elvis drove to the White House and delivered a personal letter to President Richard Nixon, requesting a meeting. This was an extremely unusual and unconventional way to approach the American President, but to the complete astonishment of everyone except Elvis, Nixon contacted the singer at his hotel and invited him to the Presidential Residence. Elvis, accompanied by Sonny West and Jerry Schilling, spent some time chatting pleasantly with Nixon, after which he asked the President whether he could have a Federal Narcotics Badge. It was an astonishing request, but even more astonishing, it was granted.

That Elvis could have been given an 'instant' audience with the President of the United States, and then been granted a Narcotics badge, was quite extraordinary, and it seems most unlikely that any other popular entertainer would have had the effrontery to even make the request, while it is equally unlikely that any other American President would have taken the request seriously. However, it must be admitted that this utterly bizarre occurrence provides a perfect example of just how special and unique a person Elvis was considered, even by the most powerful man in the United States, although both Presley and Nixon would be seen rather differently before the end of the decade.

STILL THE KING

Live stage appearances dominated Elvis Presley's career during the Seventies in much the same way as films had been the major factor of the Sixties. Las Vegas became the focal point during two months of every year, as thousands of Presley fans converged on the Hilton Hotel from all over the world. There were particularly strong contingents from Japan and the United Kingdom, two countries where Elvis enjoyed an even more diehard following than in his native America. He played for two full months at Vegas each year from 1970 to 1973, for two periods of two weeks each year during 1974 and 1975, and a final two-week engagement in 1976. Between these seasons there were several short tours of major American cities where Presley performed at large sports stadia and concert halls. He was accompanied by a retinue of over fifty people, including the musicians in his band, eight backing singers, a twelve-piece orchestra under the direction of Joe Guercio, a comedian, engineers, technicians, security men, drivers and friends.

Although the choice of venues with a substantial capacity meant that the sound of performances was frequently below par, they were necessary to ensure that a profit resulted after covering the large expense of the huge entourage that Elvis considered essential.

After spending most of the Sixties away from the public, Elvis was now performing more frequently than virtually every other big name entertainer – there were 156 shows during 1971, and still more, 164, in 1972, and even so he managed to sell out every night, while most shows were over-subscribed with ticket applications. The rumours continued and even increased concerning projected overseas tours for Elvis, but nothing ever materia-lized, and the foreign fans who were unable to afford a trip to the United States had to settle for two in concert movies, 'Elvis – That's The Way It Is' and 'Elvis On Tour', a satellite T.V. show from Hawaii in 1973, and a plethora of live performance albums.

These live albums, together with re-packaged compilations of old recordings, became the norm for 1970s record releases. The first live LP (the first half of the *Memphis/Vegas* double album) had been recorded at the debut seasons in Las Vegas, and was largely composed of reworkings of Elvis's early hits, but the next album, *On Stage*, recorded in Las Vegas during February 1970, and released in the following June, featured songs that were the new concert favourites, contemporary pop classics like The Beatles' *Yesterday*, Tony Joe White's *Polk Salad Annie*, John Fogerty's *Proud Mary* and Neil Diamond's *Sweet Caroline*. Following this, three of Elvis's most spectacular and widely publicized shows in New York (1972), in Hawaii (1973) and in Memphis (1974) were recorded and released in album form, and all three featured the big production sound of the Vegas shows with the band and the orchestra plus vocal support from J.D. Sumner and the Stamps, the Sweet Inspirations and Kathy Westmoreland.

In retrospect, most Elvis fans and music critics alike agree that Presley released too many live recordings during the 1970s. They wished that he could have devoted more time to work in the recording studio, especially as the on-stage soundtrack recordings featured a good deal of repetition and inevitably became as predictable and uninspiring as the movie soundtrack albums. A concept album, *Elvis Country* (subtitled *I'm 10,000 Years*

arriving unprepared at the studio and selecting the songs he would record from a pile of demo tapes. Sadly, the thought and inspiration that characterized *Elvis Country* would never be repeated. During 1971 Elvis could find the time for only a minimal amount of studio recording, the results of which were largely released on the uninspired *Elvis Sings The Wonderful World Of Christmas*, an album so lacking in adventure that it failed to feature in the charts, and as mundane as his 1957 Christmas LP had been essential.

Elvis's recorded output during the early 1970s concentrated on quantity at the expense of quality, with an average of three or four albums a year, including several hastily organized and conceptually lacklustre collections of old recordings slung together in a new sleeve. All sold respectably, and the majority made the chart, but none could compare with the multi-million selling albums released by such other acts as Bob Dylan and the Rolling Stones, who tended to concentrate on no more than one album release each year, and enjoyed a much longer run of chart success, whereas each new Presley album had the unfortunate effect of displacing its predecessor in the LP charts.

Although other acts sold more records than Elvis, none could claim as many loyal and devoted fans – the only name that might be mentioned as one which had threatened to approach the strength of Elvis's popularity was that of the Beatles, and to all intents and purposes, they were defunct by 1970. Most Elvis fans remained faithful and loyal during the first half of the 1970s, but the critics who had been so enthusiastic when he returned to live work began to turn against him, attacking him for being tired, lacking energy and gaining weight, views which in fact contained more than a grain of truth. The 'Hollywood Reporter' was particularly abrasive in comments made about a January 1971 concert, observing: 'Elvis Presley's show at the Las Vegas Hilton is sloppy, hurriedly rehearsed, uneven, mundanely lit, poorly amplified, occasionally monotonous, often silly and haphazardly co-ordinated. Elvis looked drawn, tired and noticeably heavier – weightwise, not musically – than in his last Vegas appearance'. However, the re-

Old), which was recorded in Nashville during June and September 1970, provides a tantalizing example of what might have been if only Felton Jarvis could have persuaded Elvis and the Colonel to spend less time touring and more in the studio.

Elvis Country was a collection of country standards, including *Little Cabin On The Hill*, *Make The World Go Away* (once a major hit for Eddy Arnold, Tom Parker's former client), *Faded Love* and *Funny How Time Slips Away*. Each track was followed by a segment of the song mentioned in the subtitle; *I'm 10,000 Years Old*, and the sleeve featured a faded photograph of Elvis at the age of two, wearing an ill-fitting trilby hat and a pair of dungarees. The whole package provided a rare example of a latter-day Presley LP that for once was carefully planned, in stark contrast to the vast majority that evolved almost accidentally from Elvis's habitual routine of simply

viewer also pointed out that his views were apparently not shared by the majority of the audience, who gave Presley the usual ecstatic reception.

Elvis had reached a point where he was spending more time talking to the audiences, delivering between-songs monologues that the critics particularly disliked, but which the paying customers loved. Although Elvis was one of the most photographed and admired men in the world, remarkably little was known about what he was really like, so these frequently lengthy and rambling monologues provided fascinating insights into his personality and private life. He talked of his hobbies, notably karate; the legendary 'early days'; his family and his friends. All the stories, comments and anecdotes were lapped up by the fans, who seemed far less concerned than the newspapermen that Elvis was growing older and fatter and no longer displayed such boundless energy, perhaps because the single most crucial aspect of his talent, his marvellous voice, showed no sign of deterioration, and whether tackling ballads or rockers, sacred or secular material, still remained vibrant and strong.

Elvis continued to be the number one attraction in Las Vegas – hotels were packed when he was in town, restaurants were overcrowded, and slot machines did their best business of the year. Audiences dressed up for his shows, and so did Elvis, who indulged himself with increasingly flamboyant stage costumes, studded with jewels, and with the addition of an array of capes (at Priscilla's suggestion), which he would occasionally spread giving the impression that he had grown wings! Sometimes he would wear the solid gold belt worth $10,000, which had been given to him by the management of the Hilton after his fourth season in Vegas. Despite his continuing popularity and success, however, Elvis was not a happy man, and during the last seven years of his life, he was frequently unwell, although in the early part of the decade very few outsiders were aware of it, and none of his employees seemed to realize, or perhaps were too nervous of losing their jobs to mention, just how serious his physical condition was becoming.

Illness was hampering the efforts of Felton Jarvis and RCA to cut new

Priscilla Presley leaves the Showroom at the International Hotel, Las Vegas, via the kitchens to avoid her husband's fans.

ach disorders, breathing problems and eye strain, plus the effects of increasingly large quantities of various types of 'medication' prescribed by several different doctors, perhaps in response to what seems to have been Elvis's fast-increasing hypochondria. He was taking amphetamines to help in losing weight, sleeping pills for chronic insomnia (possibly made worse by the amphetamines), and extremely powerful pain-killers for various, often minor, aches and pains. Some of these drugs had become habitual after Elvis had used them for many years, and inevitably they produced a debilitating effect on his body and his metabolism.

In addition to his health problems, Elvis suffered from acute depression, something that increased significantly after his marriage collapsed in 1972. Soon after the birth of Lisa Marie, Priscilla began to find life as Elvis's wife restricting and depressing. He did not approve of her socializing when he was absent, and as his work kept him away from home for lengthy periods, she became a virtual prisoner in either their Memphis or Los Angeles homes. Elvis would not allow Priscilla to stay with him in Las Vegas (except for opening nights) or travel with him on the road, his explanation being that 'other husbands don't take their wives to work with them', and he imposed this strict 'no wives' rule on every member of his entourage, which had the effect of severely disrupting, and in some cases destroying, the marriages of many of his companions.

Bored, starved of affection and growing more concerned and upset by her husband's life-style with his entourage on the rare occasions when she was permitted to be with him, Priscilla became increasingly desperate for something to do away from home, and after starting to take dance lessons, she began, with Elvis's encouragement, to take up his favourite sport of karate. Her karate instructor, Mike Stone, came from Hawaii, but ran a school providing tuition in the martial art in southern California. The most significant result of the lessons was that he and Priscilla were attracted to each other and became lovers. Elvis was away from home so much and so often that the couple managed to keep their relationship secret for three and a half years, and might have

studio albums, which was one of the reasons for the preponderance of live-show recordings, although it had less-obvious negative effects on his actual concerts, because he generally managed to continue performing even when he was sick and in pain – all in the best 'the show must go on' show-business traditions.

His diet caused major problems – Elvis greatly enjoyed fatty foods and frequently indulged in eating binges after a Las Vegas season or a tour, stuffing himself with his favourite high-cholesterol foods. These had the unfortunate side-effect of inflating his figure to the point where he sometimes became almost unrecognizable as Elvis Presley, the singing sex symbol, and rather more like a familiar advertising symbol for tyres. At these points he would embark on a crash diet, eating virtually nothing but slimming pills to get himself back into reasonable shape for the next series of shows. He suffered from a combination of ailments including stom-

been able to continue the clandestine affair indefinitely, had not Priscilla decided to put Elvis in the picture after discovering that he had been unfaithful to her on numerous occasions. Priscilla, apart from her disillusionment at life in the Presley camp, was most unhappy about the way in which her husband's increasingly nocturnal habits affected Lisa Marie, whom he liked to stay up with him, and was also alarmed at Elvis's growing use of drugs, and late in 1971 she told Elvis that she was leaving him and intended to live with Mike Stone.

It seemed incredible to almost everyone (including Mike Stone himself) that any woman should want to leave Elvis, one of the richest and most glamorous men in the world, for a comparatively impoverished karate instructor, and Presley was mortified. Although he tried putting on a brave face, his closest friends knew that he was desperately hurt. Ed Parker, the man who had actually introduced Priscilla to

With entertainer Glen Campbell in 1972.

An expressive moment from 'Elvis On Tour'.

Mike Stone, recounted in the book 'Inside Elvis': 'The biggest setback in his life was the death of his mother, but the biggest threat to his ego was the loss of his wife. Had Priscilla died, he could have coped, but to lose her to another man was a mortal blow. There is no way to forget the night he took me aside at his home in Beverly Hills and told me of his impending divorce. He poured out his soul that night, and I saw him cry for the first time.'

Elvis temporarily comforted himself by embarking on a massive eating spree, then tried to diet in readiness for a tour of the American south-east, which was to be filmed for his second movie documentary, 'Elvis On Tour'. The film (originally scheduled to be titled either 'Sold Out' or 'Standing Room Only') was produced and directed by Pierre Adidge and Robert Abel, who had recently completed work on another 'rock-on-the-road' movie, 'Mad Dogs And Englishmen', which chronicled a tour starring Joe Cocker and

Leon Russell. They intended that the Elvis film should concentrate on his concerts and, 'a tour of Elvis's life, a close-up of the birth and life of an American phenomenon', and extracts were included from some of the star's early T.V. appearances during the 1950s, plus a montage of film clips from the 1960s. The film-makers were amazed at the behaviour of the fans at Elvis's concerts, particularly the spectacular opening, where shows began in total darkness with the strains of *Also Sprach Zarathustra*, the Richard Strauss composition that had been used as the theme for the notable Stanley Kubrick movie '2001 – A Space Odyssey', after which Elvis appeared on stage to be greeted by rapturous applause, screams of delight and flashes from hundreds of cameras.

Elvis was out of condition during the tour, but the film makers did their best to disguise the fact – as Bob Abel told Jerry Hopkins: 'He was overweight and pale on

version of the Dennis Linde song, *Burning Love*, which reached Number Two on the American charts to become Elvis's biggest hit since *Suspicious Minds* three years before.

During June 1972, Elvis played three nights in New York City at the huge Madison Square Garden arena, and the concerts coincided with a rock'n'roll revival that had been germinating since the 1968 'comeback' T.V. show. Several big names from the 1950s had been performing in New York, but it was Elvis who attracted the biggest crowds and most press interest, and among the numerous celebrities who attended the shows were erstwhile Beatles John Lennon and George Harrison, as well as David Bowie, who had become RCA's biggest star since Elvis himself.

The concerts were extremely successful, with box-office takings marginally less than $750,000 of which Elvis's share was said to be one third, while he would make still more from the proceeds of a live album, which was rush-released to be available within days of the shows. For a change, the critics found kind words – a 'Variety' writer noted: 'Presley is now a highly polished, perfectly timed, spectacularly successful show business machine. He performed about twenty numbers with supreme confidence in a routine which was better constructed and choreographed than most Broadway musicals'.

The success of the four New York shows (there were two shows on the middle night of the three) encouraged Colonel Parker to arrange an even more spectacular event, in the shape of a concert that would be televised and transmitted around the world by satellite. The Honolulu International Center was selected as the venue, a choice recalling previous triumphs on the Hawaiian islands, such as his most successful film, 'Blue Hawaii', and the acclaimed charity concert back in 1961. Parker negotiated an excellent deal for his client whereby Elvis received a payment of $500,000 plus fifty per cent of the profits and, additionally, after just two showings on American television, the programme became Elvis's property and could be resold to whoever might want it.

The original intention had been to transmit the show live around the world

Left: Elvis faces the press in New York before his Madison Square Garden concerts, 1972.

the tour, so we lighted him carefully, using a lot of flesh tones. We used reds and ambers and golds and things like that to try and get him a better colour'. Filming began in March 1972, when Elvis was in Hollywood for his solitary recording session of the year – instead of the regular Nashville session men he was backed on this occasion by his permanent stage group, who by this time comprised James Burton and John Wilkinson on guitar, Glen D. Hardin on piano, bass player Emory Gordy and drummer Ronnie Tutt, plus vocal backing from J.D. Sumner and the Stamps.

They recorded about half a dozen songs, two of which were released together on a single at the end of the year, *Separate Ways* (co-written by Elvis's friend and bodyguard, Red West) and *Always On My Mind*, and were interpreted by fans as concerning the break-up with Priscilla, while another stand-out track cut at the sessions was a smouldering

via the Globcom satellite, but the combination of time differences and a certain lack of enthusiasm on the part of T.V. stations in some countries (including Great Britain, where it has yet to be shown on T.V.) altered these ambitious plans. Japan was the country that showed the most interest, so the show was transmitted live in that direction, broadcast from Hawaii at 12.30 a.m. local time on January 14, 1973, and watched during peak Japanese viewing time by an unbelievable ninety-eight per cent of the potential audience. Other countries were sent taped copies of the show, which were transmitted usually during the following week, while American fans were able to view it two weeks later.

Thanks to the massive T.V. exposure, the resulting double album, *Aloha From Hawaii Via Satellite*, topped the Amer-

ican LP charts, and was an international best seller. Like all Elvis's latter-day shows, the album opened with the *Also Sprach Zarathustra* theme, after which some twenty-three songs were featured, only eight of which were new to Elvis record buyers, although all eight were cover versions, including a most emotional rendering of *You Gave Me A Mountain*, James Taylor's *Steamroller Blues* and Hank Williams's country lament *I'm So Lonesome I Could Cry*. The album had the distinction of becoming the first quadraphonic release to sell more than a million copies.

July 1973, saw Elvis recording in the Stax studios in Memphis with a hybrid backing band made up of several of his regular stage musicians (including James Burton) and several of those who had featured on the productive American

Elvis disembarking at Virginia Airport in 1972. Joe Esposito (wearing glasses) and Colonel Parker are in the foreground.

Sound sessions in 1969, including Tommy Cogbill and Reggie Young. If Felton Jarvis and RCA were hoping that home-town sessions would produce similar results to those that accrued from Presley's previous recording stint in Memphis, they were due for a disappointment, as Elvis was notably overweight, had nothing prepared to record, and appeared to be extremely depressed – organist Bobby Wood later recalled, 'He just didn't seem to care'. Elvis was accompanied by several members of his entourage and allowed himself to be distracted from getting down to serious work, the result being that everyone involved found the five-day session depressing, and only twelve songs were recorded in that time, of which only *Raised On Rock* seems to have possessed any redeeming features.

One of the problems depressing Elvis was his impending divorce. Although it was Priscilla who wanted the divorce, for technical reasons it was Elvis who filed the application. She had originally told Elvis that she would not need much money, but away from the Presley family and her unlimited charge accounts for the first time since the age of seventeen, Priscilla realized that she would require a considerable sum of money for herself and Lisa Marie, and Elvis was more than happy to give her whatever she requested. On October 9, 1973, the divorce was finalized, and Priscilla received $750,000 plus $6,000 per month, as well as half the proceeds of the sale of one of their Los Angeles houses and five per cent of two of Elvis's publishing companies. The couple were photographed arm in arm outside the Santa Monica Superior Court after the divorce was granted, and seemed quite happy and, despite everything, still the best of friends. Elvis contrived to hide his acute distress from the outside world, but close acquaintances knew how he really felt – as T.G. Sheppard, now a major country music star, but at that time, RCA's Memphis promotion man, remembered, 'I saw so many hours of sadness and hurt and bewilderment – when the marriage failed, it was such a damaging blow', while according to Dee Presley, 'After he and 'Cilla broke up, he lost control'.

Elvis was relying on drugs to help him through his depressions, and this increas-

Left top: Captured during 'Aloha From Hawaii By Satellite', January 1973, and (below left) Elvis on stage later the same year.

Priscilla with Lisa Marie (aged seven).

ing dependence caused great concern to Dr. George Nichopoulos, his Memphis-based physician – just six days after the divorce, the doctor persuaded Presley to enter the Baptist Memorial Hospital in Memphis, ostensibly for treatment of 'recurring pneumonia', although, as he testified at a medical hearing some two years after Presley's death, 'I thought he was probably addicted to demerol (a pain-killing drug) at the time of his first hospitalization, and we tried to detoxify him from everything he was taking'.

The two-week stay was not successful, both because it was too brief and because the people around Elvis continued to supply him with whatever he wanted, including various pills and unsuitable foods, and as soon as he returned to Graceland, he was taking as many drugs as before. His entourage of friends and employees seem never to have questioned what they were asked to do, and as Red West later explained: 'There was little any of us wouldn't have done for him'. Rick Stanley, the teenage son of Dee Presley's earlier marriage, was by this time a key member of the entourage, and he summed up the attitude of those around Elvis in the book, 'Elvis: We Love You Tender', when he wrote: 'There were times when I protested, but in the long run, I was

only to reinstate them after a period of remorse. These times were depressing and confusing, although the entourage continued, as if everything was normal, to do just what Elvis told them. A few people did attempt to divert Elvis from his self-destructive course, including Priscilla (although she had little influence on him after the divorce), Joe Esposito and Dr. Nichopoulos, while the lawyer who had co-ordinated the divorce, Ed Hookstratten, also tried to help Elvis, and during 1973 hired private detectives John O'Grady and Jack Kelly to investigate anyone supplying Elvis with drugs and to try to scare them off. They discovered that he was being prescribed huge amounts of very powerful drugs by three different Las Vegas doctors and a dentist. Some of the prescriptions were made out to Presley's friends, but the medicines were given to their boss. Also, a West Coast medic had been injecting Elvis with a solution produced by mixing together novocaine, demerol and cortisone, telling the singer that he was undergoing acupuncture. It was this 'treatment' that had precipitated the hospital stay in October 1973 – as Dr. Nichopoulos later said 'We almost lost him then'. All the drugs had been legally prescribed, so that the detectives could do little beyond warning about the doctors, which meant that Hookstratten had minimal success. From this point on, Dr. Nichopoulos spent long periods on the road with Elvis in largely fruitless attempts to control his drug intake – Presley still managed to acquire pills from various sources, and was sometimes so befuddled by the often

Left: Elvis at the wedding of his bodyguard, Sonny West, where he was best man.

A party of Danish fans visiting Elvis's birthplace in Tupelo in 1973.

devoted to the man, to doing his bidding, and I would do whatever he wanted me to do. Whether or not it was good for his health didn't seem to make any difference'. This attitude seems to have been shared by almost everyone at Graceland, including the cooks, who had been given special diet sheets for Elvis from the doctor, but nevertheless continued to supply vast quantities of Elvis's favourite cheeseburgers, because they were afraid of losing their jobs if they didn't please their master.

The drugs would sometimes affect Elvis's behaviour, and in spasms of anger he would dismiss staff for trivial reasons,

bewildering kaleidoscope of effects they produced that from time to time he came close to overdosing.

There were several hospital visits for a variety of serious ailments and for detoxification, although none were totally successful, and even when he was occasionally weaned off one variety of drug, the cleansing of his system was only temporary. Maurice Elliot, the vice-president of the Baptist Memorial Hospital, was the man with the unenviable task of trying to convince the international array of journalists who swarmed around the hospital whenever Elvis was admitted that his illnesses were only minor. After Presley's death, he explained: 'It's common knowledge now that Elvis suffered from a number of chronic medical problems, but whenever he came in, I said he was in for a rest, or else he had the 'flu'. The effects of the drugs were now taking a devastating toll on Elvis's mind and body, and in the book 'Elvis: What Happened?', Sonny West confirmed that Elvis had become a changed person by the 1970s: 'He was no longer the shy, fun-loving kid from Memphis. No, he was just living for himself and all that damn junk food he took – he was like a walking drugstore'. Elvis spent many of his off-duty days doing nothing but lounging around Graceland and watching television – frequently bored, he developed a disturbing habit of extinguishing T.V. sets with one of his many guns. For some reason, he possessed a particular aversion to the

singer Robert Goulet, and Sonny West recounted what may have been a typical occurrence: 'One afternoon, he was eating breakfast, and on comes Robert Goulet on the big television set. Very slowly, Elvis finishes what he has in his mouth, puts down his knife and fork, picks up a .22 and – boom! – blasts old Robert clean off the screen and the television to bits'.

The live shows continued, and Elvis performed as well as possible, although he had very little enthusiasm for recording or rehearsing, but in December 1973, he was encouraged to return to the Stax Studio in Memphis. Once again, the musicians involved were depressed by the experience, but the session was rather more productive than its predecessor, and several above-average tracks were captured, including a sizzling version of Chuck Berry's panoramic journey around the United States, *The Promised Land*, which reached the American Top 20 and the British Top Ten, *My Boy*, which achieved similar chart success, and the wistful *There's A Honky Tonk Angel (Who'll Take Me Back In)*.

It would be another fifteen months before Elvis returned to a recording studio, and his next major album, released in June 1974, was yet another live concert LP, recorded at the Mid-South Coliseum in Memphis, which marked his first home-town show in many years. The resulting LP, *Recorded Live On Stage In Memphis*, was disappointing both because it included a minimum of new material

The T.V. room at Graceland, where Elvis enjoyed watching several stations simultaneously.

and because it was considerably less successful commercially than the previous live records. Because they were unable to coax sufficient new material out of Elvis, RCA dug into their vaults and emerged with one of the few genuinely imaginative repackages of their star's older material. *Elvis – A Legendary Performer. Volume 1* came complete with an illustrated booklet and featured some early classics like *Heartbreak Hotel* and *That's All Right*, a smattering of rare tracks (including previously unreleased versions of *I Love You Because*, which dated back to the Sun era, and *Are You Lonesome Tonight*), and a couple of excerpts from the 'Elvis Sails' interview recorded when Elvis embarked for Germany a decade and a half earlier. Later in 1974, RCA issued the positively dreadful *Having Fun With Elvis On Stage*, a collection of between-songs dialogue (but without any music) which was presumably still extant from one of the live albums, perhaps having been retrieved from the aural equivalent of the proverbial cutting-room floor. This album must rank as the most banal of all Presley's official releases, and was clearly an act of desperation on the part of RCA to try to tide them over until some new material might appear.

The one person who might have been able to halt Elvis's tragic slide into decline was, of course, Colonel Tom Parker. However, perhaps by design, the Colonel never became particularly involved with Presley's private life and, during the 1970s at least, was increasingly preoccupied with his own problems, which

Above: Elvis's private plane, the 'Lisa Marie'.

Backstage at Philadelphia, 1974.

Having fun onstage, 1974.

153

were apparently caused by heavy (and presumably unsuccessful) gambling. Jean Aberbach, a founder of the Hill and Range company who had known the Colonel for many years, told Albert Goldman: 'Up to the time he discovered Las Vegas, [the Colonel] was a loyal, wonderful human being. But this Las Vegas thing changed his entire personality. His gambling . . . he lost enormous amounts! He was forced to deal with the people to whom he lost the money', and this may explain why Elvis continued to perform at the Hilton, despite the vast financial inducements from other hotels in the resort city. Gambling debts could also provide a clue as to why the Colonel sold the rights to Elvis's back catalogue to RCA in 1973 for a reported $5,500,000 which effectively meant that Elvis would earn no more money from his old recordings, and partially explains why the sums received by the Elvis estate since the singer's death seem so remarkably small. It was obviously necessary for the Colonel to raise a huge sum, and while his agreement with Elvis meant that the latter would receive fifty per cent of the proceeds of the sale, it was far from a good deal for Elvis, whose net receipts after tax and other deductions have been estimated at just $750,000. While there is no evidence that Elvis felt aggrieved at this particular deal, there were a number of aspects of the partnership about which he was unhappy, and several arguments ensued during 1974, including one over the *Having Fun* album which Elvis, to his eternal credit, did not want RCA to release, and another over a television gospel show the Colonel insisted he should make. Matters came to a head when Elvis, from the stage at the Hilton, criticized the hotel's management for sacking a chef at the hotel. Parker, who had just negotiated an increase in Presley's fee for playing at the Hilton, was furious, and a blazing row ensued that ended with Elvis maintaining that they should dissolve the partnership, although by the next day he realized that he was so hopelessly entangled with the Colonel that a split would cost him a fortune – Parker tended to take his share of profits in arrear, so that Elvis always owed him large sums.

Despite the fortunes he earned from concerts, records and publishing, Elvis

always seemed to be short of money. Never one to do things by halves, he tended to go on frequent and often quite ludicrous spending sprees – one night, he purchased fourteen Cadillacs from a Memphis car showroom, one of the cars being for a black woman who just happened to be standing outside, while several members of his entourage received lavish gifts, and several surprise presents were given to his musicians and singers, often after he had been rude to them on stage or arrived late for a rehearsal. Linda Thompson, his main girlfriend between 1972 and 1976, received many gifts, and both her parents and her brother were given new homes.

Elvis also bought several aircraft – at one point in 1974/5, he had five, including a sixteen-seater Jet Star, which the Colonel utilized when he was setting up tours, and a luxuriously appointed Corvair 880, the Lisa Marie, which carried Elvis and his closest staff between dates. When Elvis heard that singer John Denver had bought a Rolls-Royce car for his manager, he decided to go several times better, and bought the Colonel a million-dollar Gulfstream, although Parker, who knew that this was one luxury Elvis really could not afford, refused the offer. Jewellery was one of Presley's great weaknesses, and he spent millions of dollars on precious stones, often to give them as presents to others. Lowell Hays, a Memphis jeweller who from time to time travelled with Elvis, estimates that the singer spent at least a million dollars with him, while a Beverly Hills dealer says that Elvis paid him $500,000, and on one unforgettable evening in North Carolina, Elvis reacted to the rather frosty reception of his audience by giving away some $35,000 worth of stones and rings.

Vernon Presley continued to look after his son's financial affairs, and travelled to most shows, but still found the problem of coping with Elvis's spending quite horrendous. Dr. Nichopoulos told Stanley Booth: 'Elvis and his father didn't see eye to eye on a lot of business things they did together . . . . Elvis was always spending more than he was taking in, and it was always driving his father crazy, but Elvis figured that if he spent all the money in his bank account, then he could do another tour and make more.'

With another American President, this time Jimmy Carter, and his wife, during the mid-1970s.

There were several short tours during 1975, but first, Elvis went into the RCA Studios in Hollywood to finally cut some new material. The twelve-day session produced only ten songs, although several were of reasonable quality, including *I Can Help*, written by country singer and former Graceland gateman Billy Swan, *T.R.O.U.B.L.E.*, *Shake A Hand* and a version of *Green Green Grass Of Home*, originally recorded by country star Porter Wagoner and also a big hit during the mid-1960s for Elvis's chum Tom Jones. All were featured on *Elvis Today*, the last and best of the three 1975 album releases by Presley apart from budget reissues, of which there were several.

After the studio session, Elvis played the inevitable two weeks in Las Vegas, and then began another round of short tours, although he rarely knew which town or city he was in, and each day passed in a blur. He would arrive at a hotel where his retinue would have already taken over a complete floor and covered the windows with aluminium foil – the organization was extremely slick and professional, and guitarist John Wilkinson once said, 'It was the smoothest operation I ever experienced, before or since'. Each performance ended with Elvis being whisked away in a limousine as the cheers resounded around

Below left: Fooling around onstage, May 1975.

Below right: Lavish stage costumes could not disguise the growing weight problem in June 1975.

the stadium or concert hall, and a voice announced 'Elvis has left the building', and he would go straight to the local airport and fly to the next town where another hotel was already prepared and waiting for him.

However, Elvis's physical condition was growing worse. His weight problem was now out of control and he could no longer slim down properly for tours, although he did his best to hide his increasing girth in loose-fitting costumes. His various illnesses began to affect his shows, and the summer season in Las Vegas had to be cancelled after two days, after which he flew home to Memphis and was admitted to the Baptist Memorial Hospital suffering from liver failure, severe stomach pains and an enlarged colon. He was paying the price for his ridiculous diet, and according to Sonny West, 'He would eat whole gigantic cakes by himself. He would get mad at us after he ate the stuff, and if we hid it from him, he'd get mad again. He was very fat and had a lot of problems with his stomach not working – the pills were doing all the work'.

In December, 1975, Elvis returned to Las Vegas for an extra season to replace the cancelled dates, and while the last month of the year is traditionally the worst

for business in the resort city, he played to packed houses, and there was no question that, at least in the eyes of the public, he was still The King. The year ended with a ludicrous event, but one packed with Presley fans. He took his Las Vegas show to play at a vast open-air stadium in Pontiac, Michigan, on New Year's Eve. The weather was freezing, the musicians had to wear coats to keep themselves warm enough to play their instruments properly, and it was an ultimately unpleasant and uncomfortable experience for all concerned. The only motive for staging the show had been to make money; to that end it was a great success, as the box office grossed $816,000, a record for a single concert in Detroit.

The new year opened with RCA as desperate as ever for new material from their fading superstar, and in its absence they compiled two further enterprising reissues. The second volume of *Elvis – A Legendary Performer* featured some of his best-known tracks that had been hits, several rare recordings, including the previously unknown *Harbour Lights*, which dated from the Sun days, and had been discovered on a tape among the personal effects of Steve Sholes after the latter's death, and a pair of interview extracts. Two months after the release of

this album, in March 1976, came *The Sun Sessions*, an album containing the vast majority of Presley's recordings for Sam Phillips in 1954/5.

When they realized that it was unlikely that they would be able to persuade Elvis back into either their Nashville or Hollywood studios, RCA decided to take recording equipment and musicians to Elvis's Graceland mansion, and a first home-studio session took place in early February, shortly before nine months of short tours. A selection of bluesy ballads were recorded, as these seemed to be the only type of song Elvis was inclined to perform. Among the tracks cut were *Hurt, I'll Never Fall In Love Again* and *Solitaire*. The resulting LP, *From Elvis Presley Boulevard, Memphis, Tennessee,* was one of the singer's least successful, although the best song from the session, *Moody Blue*, was saved for release as a single, and topped the country charts at the end of the year.

Elvis reportedly behaved abnormally during the session – unhappy about the

Above: Elvis arriving with his entourage at yet another airport, 1976.

Below: Onstage, summer 1975.

sound, he had to be physically restrained from destroying some of the loudspeakers with a loaded shotgun which he had brought with him, and even insiders were now very alarmed by his physical and mental condition. John O'Grady, the detective who had been hired to check up on the doctors who were supplying Presley with drugs, realized that Elvis would certainly die before long if he were not separated from his 'medication', and contacted lawyer Ed Hookstratten, after which they worked with Priscilla Presley to try to get Elvis admitted to an exclusive clinic in San Diego where he could 'dry out'. Priscilla did her best to persuade her ex-husband to enter the clinic, but he refused, being quite unwilling to accept that he might have a drug problem.

From that point on, it was downhill all the way. Elvis was now suffering from a frightening array of medical disorders, including blood clots in his swollen legs, hypoglycaemia, an enlarged heart, glaucoma, breathing problems and an expanded and distended colon, and although he submitted to occasional periods of rest and hospitalization, they never lasted sufficiently long to do anything more than slow his decline temporarily. His visibly failing health and increasingly unbalanced behaviour had a depressing effect on his companions, several of whom had seen their own private lives crumble due to the pressures of working with Elvis. The wives of Alan Fortas, Lamar Fike, Joe Esposito and Sonny West had all left home because their husbands were so frequently absent, and Vernon Presley suffered a near-fatal heart attack after Dee left him because he was away from home so much.

Several of Presley's closest friends left his employment, including Gene Smith, Richard Davis and Alan Fortas, and so did some of the musicians. Both Glen D. Hardin and James Burton began working with country singer Emmylou Harris in her celebrated Hot Band, although Burton always made himself available when Elvis needed him, and Hardin's replacement, pianist David Briggs, eventually went to work in Nashville. The musicians tended to see the worst side of Elvis, a side of which the public was still largely unaware – Tony Brown recalled an occasion when Presley arrived for a concert

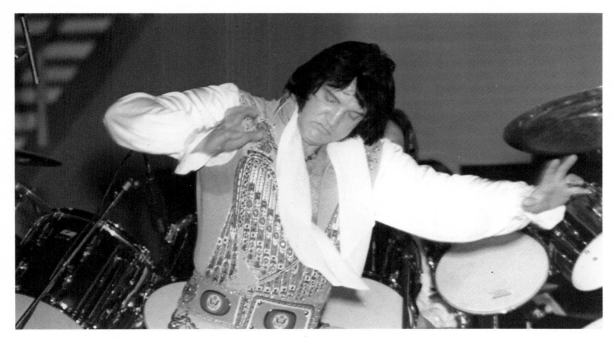

Elvis enjoyed a remarkable relationship with his audiences, despite his failing faculties. The photographs on this and the opposite page were taken by fans from the audiences at his 1976 shows.

159

unable to stand: 'He fell out of the limousine onto his knees, and when he got on stage, he held on to the mike stand as if it was a post. Everybody was scared. . . .'

Linda Thompson, who had been Elvis's girlfriend for four years, left him in 1976. After his death, she explained: 'He could have died any number of times during the years I spent with him. When a person knocks himself out each night with sleeping pills, he's just as apt to fall asleep face down on the floor as he is to be tucked away in bed when the medication hits. For that reason, Elvis required an unfathomable amount of attention. He had a self-destructive vein, and I couldn't watch him self-destruct'.

In October, another three-day session took place at Graceland, when more slow and bluesy songs were recorded, including *Way Down*, which became a huge British hit during the following year, *Pledging My Love* and *He'll Have To Go*, all of which appeared on *Moody Blue*, the last album released during Presley's lifetime. The first month of 1977 was a rest period for Elvis, but each of the next five months saw him embarking on short tours. There were no more studio recording sessions, but some shows were recorded by Felton Jarvis in April, and June concerts in Omaha and Rapid City were filmed and recorded for a scheduled CBS-T.V. Special. Elvis looked very ill, was desperately overweight and sweated continuously, and during *Are You Lonesome Tonight*, a song he must have performed several hundred times, he forgot his words.

Elvis gave his final concert performance at Indianapolis on June 26, 1977, after which he returned to Memphis to relax with his new girlfriend Ginger Alden, and his daughter, Lisa Marie, who was on her longest visit to Graceland since leaving with her mother in 1972. A further tour was scheduled to begin on August 17. While he was at home at Graceland, Elvis received an advance copy of 'Elvis: What Happened?' a book written by Red and Sonny West and Dave Hebler with a journalist. The former trio had been dismissed by Vernon Presley from the entourage because it was claimed that they had attracted bad publicity to the Presley camp with their rough treatment

of people trying to get to Elvis backstage and at a hotel. The book provided the first inside account of the darker side of Elvis's private life, and particularly of his drug taking. Elvis was depressed and annoyed by what he saw as their betrayal. When Sonny West was asked what he thought Elvis's reaction to the book would be, he said: 'He'll get hopping mad at us, because he'll know that every word is true . . . but maybe, just maybe, it'll do some good'. The book was published, amid widespread publicity on August 1, 1977, just fifteen days before Elvis died.

Presley woke up around four o'clock in the afternoon on August 15, ate breakfast, then played for a while with Lisa Marie, and that evening, he visited his dentist, Dr. Lester Hoffman, with Ginger Alden, and received two fillings. Back at Graceland in the floodlit court behind his house, he and Ginger and Billy and Jo Smith played two games of racquet ball, which Dr. Nichopoulos had suggested he take up to help with the weight problem, and at about 6.00 a.m. the next morning he and Ginger retired to bed. Elvis couldn't sleep, so he read for a while, before calling Rick Stanley to bring him his usual sleeping pills, of which there were eight, including quaaludes, seconal, tuinal,

160

A fan's grasping hand reaches for the ultimate trophy, one of Elvis's scarves.

amytal, valium and demerol. Despite this dosage, which would have proved lethal for most people, he was still unable to sleep, so he telephoned a nurse at Dr. Nichopoulos's office, and called for more pills, which was not such an unusual occurrence, as he frequently woke up and took further huge doses of 'medication' to return him to oblivion.

Ginger awoke at 2.00 p.m. in the afternoon of August 16 and discovered that she was alone in bed, so went looking for Elvis, whom she found in the bathroom doubled up and face down on the floor. She immediately summoned help, and Joe Esposito, who rushed upstairs, saw that Elvis was in an extremely serious condition and telephoned for an ambulance as well as attempting mouth-to-mouth resuscitation. Dr. Nichopoulos arrived immediately after the ambulance, and travelled with his patient to the Baptist Memorial Hospital, repeatedly shouting during the eight-minute journey, 'Breathe Elvis . . . come on, breathe for me'. But Elvis was dead, and had probably been so for some time. After thirty minutes of fruitless attempts to revive him, Dr. Nichopoulos emerged from the hospital's emergency department and told Joe Esposito and Charlie Hodge, 'It's over, he's gone'. The tragic news was withheld from the press for half

an hour, while the doctor returned to Graceland to inform Vernon, and at 3.30 p.m., the announcement was made.

The story was front-page news around the world. Elvis Presley was dead at the age of forty-two. Radio stations interrupted their normal programmes and played Elvis records, and within hours, fans began travelling towards Memphis from all parts of the United States. A huge crowd gathered outside Graceland, standing in silent mourning, in a public display of grief unequalled since the death of President John F. Kennedy, who had been assassinated in November 1963. During the evening, the coroner, Jerry Francisco, gave a press conference to announce his preliminary findings. Presley's death, according to Francisco, was due to 'cardiac arrhythmia' which, he explained, was another name for a heart attack. He said there was no indication of drug abuse, and that the only traces of drugs found were those prescribed by the doctor for hypertension and a stomach complaint. Francisco noted: 'There was a severe cardiovascular disease present, and he had a history of mild hypertension and some coronary artery disease. These two diseases may be responsible for cardiac arrhythmia, but the precise cause was not determined, and basically, it was a natural death. It may take several days or it may take several weeks to determine the cause of death, but the precise cause of death may never be discovered'.

Subsequent revelations about Elvis's drug habits do tend to make nonsense of the suggestion that he died a 'natural death'. These revelations were supported by the disclosure of a post-mortem report by a pathologist at the Bioscience laboratory in Van Nuys, California, who had been sent tissue samples from Elvis's body and reported that traces of thirteen different drugs were found, including a concentration of codeine ten times greater than the toxic level. When other pathologists were shown copies of this report by a T.V. investigator, all agreed that Elvis's death was probably due to polypharmacy – a combination of many different drugs – but the exact cause of death has never been definitely established and published. The complete autopsy report, requested by Vernon Presley, was not published and is protected by a fifty-year 'privacy' rule.

A quiet moment from one of Elvis's final shows.

162

THE LEGEND LIVES ON

Elvis's death proved the remarkable accuracy of Colonel Parker's proud boast that his client was 'The Greatest Entertainer In The World', and the news of his passing exerted a profound effect on literally millions of people around the world. Inevitably, the initial thrust came in and around Memphis – the crowd surrounding Graceland continued to grow, swelled by the ranks of journalists and T.V. crews. Ironically, Caroline Kennedy, daughter of the assassinated American President, had been assigned to cover the event, which can only be seen as a very shrewd move on the part of 'Rolling Stone' magazine, who had commissioned her to write her account of the aftermath of Presley's death. Perhaps the most telling newspaper headline would be published the following day – the 'Memphis Press-Scimitar' of August 17 bore a front-page lead headed by the words 'A Lonely Life Ends On Elvis Presley Boulevard'. It had been less than six years since the southern portion of Bellevue Street (in fact, the thoroughfare was also known as Highway 51 South) had been renamed Elvis Presley Boulevard by the City of Memphis, and, incidentally, had become the only major street in the United States without any identifying street signs, as souvenir-hunters had appropriated the signs and their replacements as soon as they were erected.

Radio stations and newspapers throughout the country were effectively put out of action, since their switchboards were jammed by the public asking for confirmation of the news most had heard on the radio during the afternoon, and an interesting result of CBS/T.V. News relegating the story to a relatively minor position in their evening bulletin resulted in the News show, which had dominated the ratings for many years, receiving its lowest audience figure for a decade as impatient viewers switched to other channels to have their worst fears confirmed. Many radio stations began to programme Elvis records through the night, and almost every popular musician performing in America that night mentioned that The King was dead.

While the response to his demise was predictably immense in America, it was even greater in Britain, where Elvis's continued absence from live performance had preserved for him a unique position – a few years earlier a new weekly music paper, 'National Rock Star', was launched with the 'exclusive news' (which was kept from even the executives of the paper – with the exception of the editor), that Elvis was at last planning to tour in Britain. Of course, it didn't come to anything, and neither, as luck would have it, did 'National Rock Star', which folded not long afterwards.

The news of Elvis's death was broken in Britain at the very end of one of the evening's main T.V. news bulletins, 'News At Ten', by newscaster Reginald Bosanquet, who announced, 'I have just been informed that Mr. Elvis Presley has died in Memphis, Tennessee'. Inevitably, anyone in Britain requiring information of Presley's death tried to contact Todd Slaughter, secretary of the Official Elvis Presley Fan Club of Great Britain, with the result that the telephone exchange in the Midlands city of Leicester, where Slaughter lived, was jammed for a considerable period. It should be noted that Slaughter was responsible to a large extent for keeping the name of Elvis alive in Britain. The membership of the Fan Club reportedly increased by 300 per cent in the two years after Presley's death.

ELVIS
AARON
PRESLEY

JANUARY 8, 1935
AUGUST 16, 1977

SON OF
VERNON ELVIS PRESLEY
AND
GLADYS LOVE PRESLEY
FATHER OF
LISA MARIE PRESLEY

HE WAS A PRECIOUS GIFT FROM GOD
WE CHERISHED AND LOVED DEARLY.

HE HAD A GOD-GIVEN TALENT THAT HE SHARED
WITH THE WORLD. AND WITHOUT A DOUBT
HE BECAME MOST WIDELY ACCLAIMED:
CAPTURING THE HEARTS OF YOUNG AND OLD ALIKE

HE WAS ADMIRED NOT ONLY AS AN ENTERTAINER,
BUT AS THE GREAT HUMANITARIAN THAT HE WAS;
FOR HIS GENEROSITY. AND HIS KIND FEELINGS
FOR HIS FELLOW MAN.

HE REVOLUTIONIZED THE FIELD OF MUSIC AND
RECEIVED ITS HIGHEST AWARDS.

HE BECAME A LIVING LEGEND IN HIS OWN TIME,
EARNING THE RESPECT AND LOVE OF MILLIONS.

GOD SAW THAT HE NEEDED SOME REST AND
CALLED HIM HOME TO BE WITH HIM.

WE MISS YOU, SON AND DADDY. I THANK GOD
THAT HE GAVE US YOU AS OUR SON.

VERNON PRESLEY

Above: Todd Slaughter, President of the Official Elvis Presley Fan Club of Great Britain (right), with other Presley associates, June 1977.

Right: The Elvis Presley Memorial Chapel in Tupelo, Mississippi.

The story was front-page news in every British newspaper on the day after Elvis died, and remained a major story for the remainder of the week, one notable quote (by Peter Clayton) appearing in the following weekend's 'Sunday Telegraph', which summed up the feelings of many of the British faithful: 'If you can imagine Rudolph Valentino, Marilyn Monroe, James Dean, Mario Lanza, Judy Garland and Bix Beiderbecke all combined into one corporate super tragi-star, you will get at least some idea of his hold on those to whom he belonged. What has died is the adolescence of an entire generation.' Todd Slaughter himself was quoted as saying: 'When Elvis burst upon the scene, he was to England the arrival of the American dream', which was equally accurate.

Among the tributes from notable fellow Americans were those from President Jimmy Carter, whose office issued a statement which began: 'Elvis Presley's death deprives our country of a part of itself. He was unique and irreplaceable'. Frank Sinatra was quoted as saying, 'We lost a good friend today' and Pat Boone noted: 'There's no way to measure the impact he made on society or the void that he leaves. He will always be the King of rock'n'roll'. Of course, there were some with apparently different views, such as the anonymous show-business cynic reported as saying, 'Good career move', and some of those who were close to Presley were saddened but hardly surprised by the news, like Jordanaire Ray Walker, who was quoted in the 'Memphis Press-Scimitar' as saying: 'His death wasn't really sudden – he had been in bad health for the past two or three years'.

The general disbelief that the seemingly immortal Elvis had died was expressed by a member of the huge crowd outside Graceland, who told reporters that everyone was saying that someone would come out and tell the waiting crowd that it was all a big mistake.

The following day, at noon, the body was returned to Graceland, and was put on display in its seamless copper casket. Elvis was dressed in a white suit, and the waiting fans were allowed into the mansion from 3.00 p.m. until 6.30 p.m. to see their hero lying 'in state'. 20,000 people filed past during the three and a half hours. Cameras were forbidden, but evidently someone smuggled one in, and a photograph of Elvis in his coffin appeared a few days later in the 'National Enquirer'. At the end of the procession, several fans continued to wait outside Graceland for another night, and at 4.00 a.m., an inebriated driver swerved in and out of the waiting crowd, injuring several people and killing two teenage girls. The driver, Treatise Wheeler III, was charged with drunken driving and second degree murder.

The funeral took place the same day (August 18), and over 3,000 floral tributes arrived, exhausting the entire stocks of all the florists in Memphis, and in addition, including several tons of flowers airlifted from California and Colorado. The funeral took place at 2.00 p.m. in the music room at Graceland, and was attended by 150 people, including Priscilla, Vernon and Lisa Marie, who sat in the front row, and several former employees and friends, including Linda Thompson, Ginger Alden and Ann-Margret, while Colonel Parker, in shirt sleeves, sat in the back row. The service included musical tributes, among them Kathy Westmoreland singing *My Heavenly Father Watches Over Me* and James Blackwood, with the Stamps, performing *How Great Thou Art*, the title track of Elvis's 1967 gospel LP,

The crowd watching the dedication of the Elvis Aaron Presley Highway, 1977.

and an address was given by the pastor of a nearby church, C.W. Bradley, a long-time family friend. From Graceland, a procession led by a silver Cadillac, followed by a white Cadillac hearse, and with numerous additional Cadillacs carrying the mourners, proceeded to Forest Hill Cemetery, a mile and a half along Elvis Presley Boulevard, where Gladys Presley was already buried. It has been reported that at least 50,000 people passed through the cemetery during the day, and by the time the gates were closed, hardly a single flower remained on the tomb. During the succeeding month, at least another million visitors came to pay their respects, severely stretching the cemetery's resources. Vernon Presley was most concerned about security at Forest Hill, and after three men had been arrested for trespassing, and it was suggested that they intended to steal Elvis's corpse and hold it to ransom, he sought permission to exhume the bodies of his wife and son and re-inter them at Graceland. On October 2, 1977, after permission had been granted, the bodies were moved to the Meditation Gardens within Graceland.

Despite the death of his client, Colonel Tom Parker moved with typical speed and business acumen. His first move was to contact Vernon Presley, within minutes of hearing the news, to explain that Elvis's interests, even in death, needed protection, and asking for Vernon's agreement to assign world-wide rights for Elvis souvenirs to a single company to ensure that there could be no outbreak of cheap pirated mementoes. On behalf of Boxcar Enterprises, the Tennessee company which licensed Presley souvenirs and jointly owned by himself and Elvis, he contacted Factors Inc., a powerful merchandising company, and arrived at a swift agreement with them, for which he received a $150,000 guarantee plus a royalty on each individual item sold. One curious ramification of the agreement was that Parker himself received fifty per cent of the proceeds, while the remaining fifty per cent was shared by the Presley estate and by Boxcar Enterprises, the result being that the Colonel received something in excess of fifty per cent of the gross, while the assignment to Factors Inc. also meant that the Colonel himself would not have to be involved in legal proceedings against manufacturers and sellers of pirated merchandise.

With regard to his records, the prime items of Presley merchandise, sales around the world, but especially in the United States and Britain, were phenomenal, and all stocks of Presley records in shops were sold within hours of the news of his death being confirmed. Pressing plants were pushed into action by RCA Records, with the result that the company supposedly achieved its most profitable year in 1977. In Britain, sales of Presley records reached a peak that had never previously been achieved, as nine Elvis singles (including the just previously released *Way Down* which had entered the chart a few days before he died, and which was at Number One by September 3) featured simultaneously in the charts.

In the United States, six Presley LPs were listed in the Top 100 by October 1 – even the four-album boxed set, *Worldwide 50 Gold Award Hits Volume 1* reached the Top 50, while both volumes 1 and 3 of *Elvis' Golden Records* reached the Top Three in response to his death – 'good career move' could certainly be seen to be accurate.

It wasn't only Colonel Parker and RCA Records who were able to turn a substantial profit from Elvis's demise – various branches of the media, including

television, the cinema and predominantly the book trade, began to produce Elvis memorabilia, largely in the guise of an insider spilling the beans (to a greater or lesser extent) about their late friend/employer/relative. It seems curious that few, if any, of these 'exposés' resulted in lawsuits, but perhaps Colonel Parker, who was by this time in complete command of the posthumous Presley industry, was well aware that more ammunition to fuel the fire of controversy would only increase sales of 'legitimate' Elvis merchandise. The one person who might have been able to inhibit the Colonel's money-making activities, Vernon Presley, seems to have taken little, if any, exception to Parker's plans, perhaps because he was a major beneficiary in his son's will, the main clauses of which left the remains of the Presley fortune to Vernon and Elvis's grandmother, Minnie Mae Presley, and to Lisa Marie, who would inherit everything when she reached the age of twenty-five.

The two years following Elvis's death saw Colonel Parker receiving a massive income not only from merchandising – it has been said that more than 20 million dollars was spent on Presley souvenirs during the first year of posthumous activity – but also from the sale of rare film clips to the makers of documentaries, and even from the somewhat obnoxious concept of 'Elvis wine', authorized by the Colonel, of course, and with a bottle whose label showed not only a picture of Elvis, but also contained a poem written about Elvis by the Colonel, for which the latter was reportedly paid a royalty of $28,000, a sum of which most poets would not dare to dream! Equally tasteless was another event, co-produced by Parker and Vernon Presley, the 'Always Elvis' festival held in Las Vegas at the Hilton Hotel, where Elvis had performed so often during his lifetime. A life-size bronze statue of the singer was unveiled by Priscilla Presley and stood in a glass case outside the renamed Elvis Presley Showroom, the auditorium in which Elvis had performed, while situated in another part of the hotel was an exhibition of Elvis's stage costumes and personal effects. Albert Goldman reported that what typified the event as being conceived by Colonel Parker was the fact that the paying public were expected to pay as much to see a statue of Elvis and some personal paraphernalia as they had paid to see him perform in previous years.

On August 16, 1978, the first anniversary of Elvis's death, many fans congregated in Memphis where a series of Presley films were shown and numerous 'memorial events' were planned. However, the anniversary coincided with a major strike by the local police force, as a result of which a curfew was imposed and many of the 'events' were cancelled. It was yet another example of how little the memory of Elvis was regarded by his adopted home town, even though numerous Memphians were numbered among his fans. While the City Council often spoke of commemorating the fact that most of Presley's life was spent in the city, very little occurred in concrete terms, and most suggestions were dropped before they had passed the planning stage. For some years, the best tour of Memphis available to visiting Presley fans was organized by Gray Line Coaches, who at least made some attempt to restore the Sun Recording Studio, which they acquired after it had been used first as a paint shop and later as a car repair workshop, and also pointed out to tourists several of Elvis's early homes and schools.

It would not be until the 1980s that matters of this nature would improve,

perhaps to a great extent because control of the Presley Estate (and some appreciation of how little money it was generating) passed to Priscilla Presley after Vernon died of a heart attack during June 1979. Control of the Estate then became virtually vested in Lisa Marie, Minnie Mae being in her late eighties (she would also die soon afterwards, in May 1980), and Priscilla was Lisa Marie's legal guardian. Perhaps unsurprisingly, Colonel Parker's relationship with Priscilla was less amicable than had been the virtual omnibus acquiescence of Vernon, and some improvements were made relating to facilities for visiting fans. It wasn't until June 7, 1982, that Graceland was finally opened to the public, although the gardens had been available to the public for some time beforehand. The mansion had been turned into a memorial museum, with guided tours around the house and grounds. Admission prices were five dollars for adults and three dollars for children, and it was reported in the 'Daily Mirror' a few weeks before the tours started that the executors of the Presley Estate needed extra finance to meet running costs. Two years before, on the anniversary of his death in 1980, a portion of Beale Street in Memphis had been named Elvis Presley Plaza, and a nine-foot high statue of Elvis cast in bronze unveiled. Even if there had been little in the way of Elvis memorials in the immediate wake of his death, they were gradually erected as time passed.

Somewhat surprisingly, it seems to

Elvis's cousin Billy poses by the pool table in Graceland. Note the opulent furnishings.

have occurred to very few Presley fans that Elvis's death was due to other than at least fairly natural causes, but in September 1979, this faith was largely shattered when Geraldo Rivera, an ex-policeman turned T.V. reporter, alleged on the ABC Network's '20/20' show that it had been drug abuse that had killed Elvis rather than a heart attack, and suggested that his death had been due to the excessive quantities of drugs prescribed by three doctors, including Dr. George Nichopoulos, 'Dr. Nick'. Perhaps as a result of Rivera's allegations, which had been leaked prior to the screening of the '20/20' programme, Nichopoulos was charged by the governing medical body in Tennessee of over-prescribing and/or illegally prescribing drugs, and according to Neal and Janice Gregory's most informative book, 'When Elvis Died', a televised hearing in January 1980 produced the information that Nichopoulos had prescribed incredible quantities of tablets for Presley between the start of 1976 and his death, as a result of which the doctor was suspended from practising for three months and sentenced to a similar period of probation. Later, during the final

quarter of 1981, Nichopoulos was tried on charges of illegally prescribing drugs, but was acquitted – it has been suggested by Elvis biographer Albert Goldman that this may have been partially at least due to the fact that the doctor's defence was conducted by the eminent James Neal, whose most notable legal commission up to this point had been as prosecutor in the celebrated Watergate scandal, which resulted in Richard Nixon resigning his presidency. Despite the doctor's acquittal, the suggestion that Elvis had died as a result of drug abuse was sown in many minds and, as we shall see, was just the first of its type.

What may be seen as an even greater threat to the Presley myth – at the time of writing it had not been legally settled – came when an attorney appointed by the Memphis probate court produced a lengthy report on the way the Presley Estate had been managed, apparently in response to a petition that was being presented by the Estate's executors seeking the court's approval of the Estate's business dealings with Colonel Parker. It was presumed that this approval was a necessary preliminary to the establish-

Part of Elvis's collection of cars and motorcycles on display at Graceland.

ment of a trust fund to which all the Estate's assets would be transferred, after which the Estate would no longer be liable to the scrutiny of outsiders.

Unfortunately, some might say, the presiding judge's attention was drawn to the vast amounts of money paid by the Estate to Colonel Tom Parker, and the judge appointed a temporary guardian for Lisa Marie, whose job it was to protect the child's interests. In simple terms, Parker was being accused of having taken far more 'commission' from Elvis, and after his death, from the Presley Estate, than he was legally entitled to deduct, and to have made private financial arrangements concerning Presley without the latter's knowledge – in short, Parker was accused of ripping off Elvis, even after his client was dead.

Inevitably, the Colonel filed a counter claim, asking the court, among other things, to ratify all his agreements with Presley, and also to stop their investigations into those agreements, as the remaining value of the Presley Estate was being diminished by the surrounding scandal. It seems likely that some parts of this litigation will be settled out of court, which leads to the supposition that full and accurate details of the financial aspects of Elvis Presley's life, and perhaps more to the point, his remarkable posthumous commercial success (the first year of which is reported to have exceeded any year of his life) will ever be available. It also seems highly likely that the opening of Graceland to the public (and the suggestion that allowing the public inside Elvis's home would provide some necessary extra money for the Estate) was not unconnected with the shortage of income resulting from Parker's seemingly excessive 'commission' – it may also be relevant to note that while a large part of the mansion, including the downstairs living quarters, is included on the 'tour', which also takes in various outbuildings such as the garage, where the 1955 pink Cadillac bought by Elvis for his mother can be seen, the upper floor, which of course, takes in Elvis's bedroom, is not included. Whether this additional attraction will one day become part of the tour (perhaps at a time when business at some point in the future has begun to flag) is a matter for conjecture.

A publicity shot from the London stage musical, 'Elvis'.

Of far wider appeal have been a number of Elvis-related films, radio and television shows and stage presentations, virtually all of which have shown the star in a favourable light. The first genuinely representative example came in the shape of a T.V. Special and double soundtrack album, which shared the title 'Elvis In Concert'. Concerts in Omaha, Nebraska, and Rapid City, South Dakota, had been filmed and recorded less than two months before Elvis died, and had he lived, would probably not have been seen or heard. However, since both the film and record were deemed, as a result of his death, to have acquired historical significance, according to Roy Carr and Mick Farren in their book, 'Elvis: The Complete Illustrated Record', both were unleashed on an unsuspecting public during October 1977. While the album seems to possess few, if any, redeeming qualities musically, the film, which was shown on T.V., seemed to show an Elvis who, despite looking very ill, was doing his best for his audiences. At the end of the film, Vernon Presley appears on screen and thanks the world for their condolences over his sad loss.

In Britain, BBC Radio One acquired the rights to broadcast a series titled 'The Elvis Presley Story', scripted by Elvis biographer Jerry Hopkins and narrated by

disc jockey Wink Martindale (who is perhaps best known in international terms for his mawkish monologue, *Deck Of Cards*, which has defied good taste by twice becoming a sizeable British hit). A somewhat more solid British contribution was the musical 'Elvis', staged by entrepreneur Jack Good, who virtually invented televised rock'n'roll, and veteran impresario Ray Cooney. Ironically, the show was conceived before Presley died, but after some heart-searching and in view of discernible public demand, it was decided to go ahead, and the play opened on November 28, 1977, at the Astoria Theatre, Charing Cross Road, with three actor/singers playing Elvis.

The idea was to tell Presley's story through his music, with the young Elvis of the Sun Records days being played by the hitherto unknown Timothy Whitnall, the mid-period Elvis of the film years by Welsh rocker Shakin' Stevens (who had been making records without much success for seven years before the 'Elvis' musical, but who later developed, perhaps as a result of his exposure in 'Elvis', into a consistent hit-maker for several years) and the latter-day, Las Vegas, Elvis by P.J. Proby, who had actually sung on demo recordings for Elvis during the early

1960s before becoming a chart star in Britain during the mid-Sixties. Proby, unfortunately, had been in the doldrums of his career before Jack Good, who had initially brought him to Britain and success, had resurrected him. According to legend, Proby had become difficult to work with – after about six months, he was replaced by Bogdan Kominowski, who had been playing the title role in another musical in London's West End, 'Jesus Christ Superstar'. 'Elvis' was a resounding success and played for several years in London, although as replacements filled the roles of the departing original actors, it gradually lost its popularity.

The same title, 'Elvis', was also used by Dick Clark, the legendary American rock'n'roll promoter, for a film he made for television that was first screened in February 1979. Vernon and Elvis Presley were played by another father-and-son acting team, Bing and Kurt Russell, and the latter was later nominated for an Emmy as best actor in a dramatic role, while other notable names in the cast included Shelley Winters as Gladys Presley and Ed Begley as Colonel Parker, while Charlie Hodge provided extra authenticity by playing himself and acting as 'technical adviser'. Another authentic

Charlie Hodge (right), a constant companion of Elvis for many years, is shown here with Bernard S. Benson, the author and illustrator of 'The Minstrel', a fable inspired by Presley.

touch was provided by Felton Jarvis, who helped to produce the singing of Elvis in the film. This was performed by Ronnie McDowell, whose own rise to fame had been dramatic – a relatively obscure country singer before Elvis died, he had sprung to fame with a tribute single, *The King Is Gone*, which sold a million copies within a week. The need for an Elvis soundalike had come about because Colonel Parker had refused to allow Dick Clark to use actual Presley recordings in the film. It was evidently a success when shown on ABC Television. While the network's two major rivals, CBS and NBC showed the noted films 'Gone With The Wind' and 'One Flew Over The Cuckoo's Nest' respectively, 'Elvis' achieved a forty-one per cent viewing audience – more than the viewing share of the other two networks combined.

In Britain, where the television audience is courted by fewer T.V. companies, the tribute came in the form of the excellent 'Long Distance Information', written by and starring Neville Smith, who played a disc jockey celebrated for his knowledge of Elvis, who also sang in a rock'n'roll band whose repertoire was composed of Presley-related songs. The play was an evocation of what had occur-red in the disc jockey's life on the night Elvis died, and when it was screened by BBC-T.V., it received justified critical praise.

Even more significant than either of these two items was 'This Is Elvis', which was effectively Elvis's thirty-fourth movie (he had appeared in thirty-three films during his lifetime) as it was not only authorized by Colonel Parker (who once again assumed the onerous role of 'technical adviser'), but also included previously unseen footage which was found, according to 'Rolling Stone' magazine, by director and writer Andrew Solt and Malcolm Leo when they first went to Graceland and happened to open a closet, out of which fell numerous movies of Elvis, some shot professionally and others of a more informal nature. The best of these, combined with more familiar footage and also out-takes from formal Presley films and T.V. shows, formed the basis of the film, although the many occasions (especially before he became famous) when cameras were not present were recreated, with no less than four Elvises as well as the genuine article, and narration by one of the first and probably the best of the Elvis soundalikes, singer Ral Donner. Inevitably, the authenticity of 'This Is Elvis'

in utilizing actual footage of Presley pushed previous biographical films into the background, despite some critics complaining that the movie contained little that was actually new.

'This Is Elvis' was premièred in Memphis on April 3, 1981, with a double album of the soundtrack concurrently released on RCA, the album containing for the first time (legally) several of Elvis's early T.V. performances on such shows as those hosted by the Dorsey Brothers, Milton Berle and Ed Sullivan. One interesting side-issue involving 'This Is Elvis' relates to the supposition (confirmed in 'Elvis: The Complete Illustrated Record') that several hours of outtakes from the film exist which could, if required, be incorporated into either a follow-up film or even, as seems to be the recent fashion, some kind of 'de luxe' edition.

While cinematic possibilities regarding Presley's story were obviously not being ignored, the amount of activity in the literary world was considerably greater. Several volumes have been acknowledged within our text, and this seems a good place to discuss the merits or otherwise of a number of the better-known books concerning Elvis that have been published, mostly since his death. One notable exception to this last condition, which was in fact published as early as 1971, is Jerry Hopkins's 'Elvis: A Biography', which was supplemented in 1980 by the same author's 'Elvis : The Final Years'. These two volumes are regarded generally as the major biographical source works relating to Elvis, and were assembled with the help of a number of 'insiders', and in particular Colonel Tom Parker, to whom Hopkins offers: 'special thanks for allowing me to clear so many fences merely by dropping his name'. To this extent, the two books by Hopkins, which are highly recommended, are the closest the world has yet seen to genuine authorized Elvis biographies. In terms of discographical information, the early 'bible' was Paul Lichter's 'The Boy Who Dared To Rock: The Definitive Elvis', which was published in the United States in 1975, but 'Elvis: The Complete Illustrated Record' by Roy Carr and Mick Farren and published in 1982, is the most up-to-date illustrated discography with

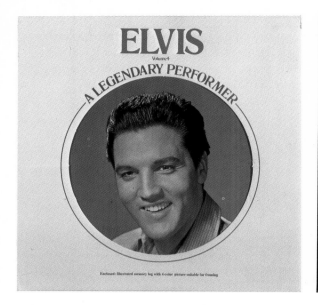

Left: RCA Records continued to issue 'new' Elvis albums after his death, although most were compilations of previous releases fleshed out with a few tracks of somewhat greater rarity.

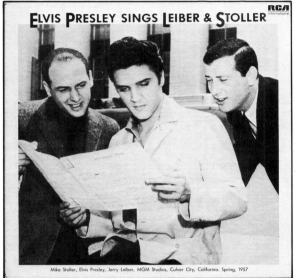

Mike Stoller, Elvis Presley, Jerry Leiber, MGM Studios, Culver City, California. Spring, 1957

recording dates, release dates and personnel and production details.

Somewhat ironically, the best-selling book about Elvis Presley is 'Elvis' by Albert Goldman, published in 1981 and popularly known as 'the only biography to tread on the blue suede shoes'. As a review in London's 'Time Out' magazine noted: 'Elvis Presley may have been the King of rock'n'roll, but the Gospel according to Goldman claims that he was also a Momma's Boy, a patsy, a narcissist, a police groupie, a drug addict, a gun worshipper, a bed-wetter, a soft drug junkie, an hysteric, a fantasist, neurotic, glutton, voyeur, prude and an accomplished wanker'. This brief summary, after which the book was obviously required reading, in fact introduced a highly critical review in the form of a lengthy article written by respected American rock critic Greil Marcus, which had originally appeared in New York's 'Village Voice' magazine. Marcus's searing indictment of the book in general and its author in particular can be summarized in one of his many snipes at Goldman: 'It seems to be Goldman's purpose to discredit Elvis Presley entirely, the culture that produced him, and the international culture he helped create – to dismiss and condemn not just Elvis Presley, but the white working-class South from which Presley came, and the pop world which emerged in Presley's wake'. While Marcus's well-considered review remains highly rated by all who approached it with a smattering of previous knowledge, it was not successful (if indeed that was its aim) in destroying sales of Goldman's book, which sold in prodigious quantities as a £10 hardback,

Opposite: 'This Is Elvis' was a composite film which included authentic footage from all stages of Presley's career plus scenes recreated using the three actors pictured here outside Graceland, who each played Elvis at a different point in his life; (left to right) Paul Boensch III, David Scott and John Harra.

175

although it is rumoured that membership of the Presley fan club, in Britain at least, plummeted as inquisitive fans discovered that, in Goldman's estimation, their idol possessed feet, if not a whole body, of clay. Opinions of the book were generally negative, although this was to a large extent cancelled out by its inability to be put down by curious readers.

Perhaps the Goldman book should have come as less of a surprise after some of the other 'kiss-and-tell' volumes that had appeared since Presley's death, the first of which was published a few days before he died, and which he actually read. 'Elvis: What Happened?' by Red West, Sonny West and Dave Hebler, as told to Steve Dunleavy, was also the first of many books written by ex-employees of Presley attempting (and in this case largely succeeding, certainly in commercial terms, as it sold around 3,500,000 copies in the weeks following its subject's death) to blow the whistle on Elvis's private life, with particular reference to his drug-taking. We shall, of course, never know whether the authors' stated aim, to prevent Elvis from killing himself by his bad habits, was in fact the major reason for the book being written, as it was evidently too late for improvement in their ex-boss' life-style. Elvis was reportedly (and not unnaturally) most upset by the book's revelations, and it remains one of the most informative accounts of life behind the walls at Graceland, even if the Wests and Hebler were feeling aggrieved at the time the book was written after having been fired by Elvis. It goes without saying that they could not possibly have suspected that Presley's death would occur so soon after the book's publication to make it such a huge success.

Several other books covered similar ground, including 'Elvis – Portrait Of A Friend' by Marty and Patsy Lacker and Leslie S. Smith, published in 1979, which is largely Marty's account of life as a member of the 'Memphis Mafia', plus a brief section contributed by his wife, who offers some extremely cutting comments on the women in Presley's life; 'Inside Elvis' by Ed Parker, Elvis's karate teacher and friend, who also, unfortunately for Elvis, was responsible for introducing Priscilla Presley to Mike Stone; and 'My Life With Elvis' by Becky Yancey and Cliff Linedecker, which tells the story from the point of view of Ms. Yancey, who was Vernon's secretary. Of somewhat greater interest because of the proximity to Elvis of its authors is 'Elvis: We Love You Tender' by Vernon's second wife, Dee Presley, and her three sons, Billy, Rick and David Stanley, as told to Martin Torgoff – Vernon never found the time to write a book before he died, and thus far, the same has applied to Colonel Parker, although 'Up And Down With Elvis Presley', written by Marge Crumbacker with Parker's erstwhile right-hand man, Gabe Tucker, provides some fascinating insights into the way the Colonel controlled Presley's career.

Away from the frequently sordid accounts of Elvis's bizarre private life, some fascinating books of photographs have surfaced, none more interesting than 'Elvis '56: In The Beginning' by Alfred Wertheimer, who was hired by RCA to shoot a photo session with their new acquitition in the very early days of Presley's recording career. Many of Wertheimer's photographs of Elvis remained unseen until 1979, nearly a quarter of a century after they were taken and, of course, after the death of their subject, apparently because the photographer failed to realize how valuable they were.

Another collection of photographs that might have severely damaged Elvis's

image and career had they been publishing during his lifetime appeared in 1978 under the title 'Private Elvis' by Diego Cortez – the pictures in this book are of Elvis and some girls (by implication, of easy virtue) taken at a German night club during his term in the U.S. Army, and the fact that they are somewhat sordid, and a long way from the clean and wholesome image that Colonel Parker was successfully promoting for his client at the time, makes it strange that the book, once again, was published posthumously – we may never know the reason why this book was delayed for so long, while it has to be said that Wertheimer's excuse – that he was unaware of how valuable his shots were – seems skimpy, to say the least. Is it possible that Colonel Parker might have been responsible for their suppression until after Elvis's death?

Several rather extraordinary books about Elvis also appeared after his death, none more strange than 'Elvis, Is That You?' by Harley Hatcher, which attempted to suggest that there were actually two Elvis Presleys, and that the singer who made all the superb records during the 1950s was substituted with a double when he was drafted into the army. It goes without saying that it was utter nonsense, but proves the point that even the most

unlikely story concerning Elvis could induce customers to part with their money. Along similar lines was 'Orion', a novel by Gail Brewer-Giorgio about an American singing star who lives in a mansion known as 'Dixieland', and who fakes his own death because of the pressures of stardom – although the book was not published until 1979, having been written some time prior to Presley's death, it added fuel to the ridiculous rumours that Elvis was still alive. To further confuse matters, a record was released on the Sun label (which by this time had been purchased from Sam Phillips by Nashville businessman Shelby Singleton, who had reactivated it after it had remained virtually dormant in terms of new releases for several years) by a mysterious masked singer named Orion. The sleeve notes with the record were calculated to produce the impression that the singer could really be Elvis, although it was actually Jimmy Ellis, one of several singers who capitalized, after Presley's death, on their ability to sing like Elvis.

Ronnie McDowell, the most successful Elvis soundalike, went on to record several more Presley style hits after *The King Is Gone*, albeit mainly directed at the country charts. In Britain, the two foremost Presley disciples (at least in terms of

Below left: Elvis impersonator Frank Chisum.

Below: Ed Parker, Presley's karate teacher and sometime bodyguard, talking to Elvis fans in Leicester, England.

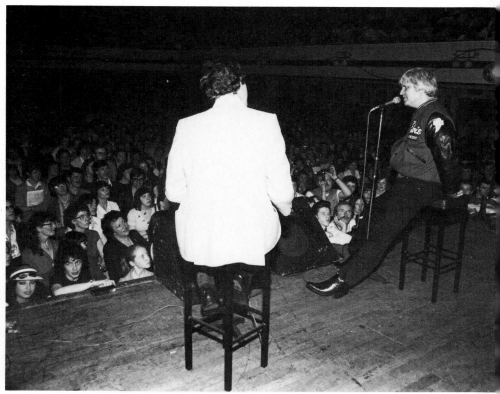

177

influence and vocal quality) have been Shakin' Stevens who, of course, played Elvis in the London stage show, and who was certainly influenced in his stage movements and garb by Presley, and Les Gray, lead singer with the group Mud, whose finest moment came with the 1974 seasonal chart-topper, *Lonely This Christmas*, which must surely qualify as the finest Christmas record in the Presley style never made by Elvis. Gray also recorded under the name of Tulsa McLean, the role played by Elvis in 'G.I. Blues'. Controversy always followed releases on the Sun label when a usually uncredited singer even vaguely resembled Elvis – a single by one '?' turned out to be nothing to do with Presley, while an album titled *Duets* by Jerry Lee Lewis, and said to date from the Fifties, although it probably did include participation from other Sun artists like Charlie Rich and even perhaps Johnny Cash, was finally revealed as including Elvis-styled vocal parts overdubbed on original Lewis tracks by Jimmy Ellis.

Which brings us to authentic posthumous Presley releases. The first notable item of this type came in the form of a third volume in the *Elvis – A Legendary Performer* series which, while it was of lesser note than the two preceding vol-

A group of Elvis imitators (of varying degrees of conviction) at an Elvis Convention at Leicester's De Montfort Hall, 1980.

umes, at least contained Elvis's version of *Danny*, a song originally designed for the 'King Creole' film, but never used. Next, and not released by RCA, but by the somewhat obscure (and not over-modest) Very Wonderful Golden Editions company, came *Elvis, Scotty & Bill – The First Year*, one side of which contained five live tracks recorded in Texas during 1955, plus a couple of interviews, and the other a description by Scotty Moore of the events of that first year on the road. Given that the album's sound quality was suspect, to say the least, the LP is a valuable early document, which unfortunately is more than can really be said for RCA's

eight LP boxed set, released in a 'limited edition' of 250,000 under the title *Elvis Aron Presley*, and to commemorate, in addition to his death, the fact that he had been signed to RCA for a quarter of a century.

With regard to the content of the eight LPs: although much of the material was unreleased, at least officially, a good deal of it was little different from what was already available (with particular reference to one and a half LPs of a 1975 concert and also an album of Las Vegas performances), while an LP of alternate takes of songs from the films was hardly indispensable. In reality, only two of the

Below: Two photographs taken during the British fan club's 'Memorial Tour To Memphis', 1980, which was the subject of a T.V. documentary presented by David Frost.

eight LPs contain notable material, in the form of a live recording of Elvis's first visit to Las Vegas in 1956 (a less than triumphant occasion) and a 1961 concert in Hawaii, performed as a benefit show in memory of the U.S.S. *Arizona*, plus a thirteen-and-a-half minute monologue by Elvis, taped on a film set during the early 1960s. Despite its shortcomings (and relatively poor value, with a running time of less than four and a half hours over eight LPs – the material could easily have appeared on five LPs), the set was apparently oversubscribed before it was even released. No doubt something similar will appear in the future.

Of equally dubious value was the 1981 LP *Guitar Man*, where Felton Jarvis (who in fact died during the same month, January, as the record's release) 'unmixed' the backings from ten Presley recordings to leave just Elvis's voice, to which he added newly recorded and supposedly less-dated musical accompaniment. While this technique had been used with some success to provide producer Norman Petty with several posthumous Buddy Holly hits, it was far less effective in Presley's case, an obvious example of the potential pitfalls being the title track, where Jerry Reed's trademark guitar style was replaced by a new backing, which was certainly more modern, but infinitely less interesting and effective. Otherwise, apart from the previously mentioned *Million Dollar Quartet* recording released in Britain during 1981, most of the significant 'new' Presley releases were conceived and executed in Britain, including two sets of EPs, each including one record's worth of rarities, and packaged in their original sleeves, and the highly recommended *Elvis Presley Sings Leiber & Stoller*, which set a precedent by allowing someone other than the star (i.e. the two songwriters) to share the front sleeve photography with Elvis, and additionally contained twenty of the best songs he ever recorded. One less-pleasing aspect of RCA's British activity is in releasing about forty Elvis albums at a budget price, supposedly to ensure that virtually everything he recorded remained available. While the idea was certainly laudable, it seems to have also devalued Presley's work to a great extent.

One other interesting LP released by RCA is *The Elvis Collection*, a 1981 LP containing versions of songs also recorded by Elvis (including tracks by Arthur Crudup and Jerry Reed), or about Elvis (such as *Tupelo Mississippi Flash* by Jerry Reed and *All American Boy* by Bill Parsons, a pseudonym for Bobby Bare). No doubt this will not be the last album conceived around the subject of Elvis.

In conclusion, there can be no doubt that Elvis was the single most important entertainer of the twentieth century, obviously because of his extraordinary talent, but also to some extent because he arrived at a point in time when youth culture needed and was searching for someone exactly like him. We shall surely never see his like again. Let us also consider Elvis as a pioneer, perhaps in musical terms (although this is a matter for much conjecture) but certainly in respect of the fact that he was the first popular singer of the post Second World War era to excite such fervour in his fans. Elvis, with no example to copy, decided (or was advised) that the best thing he could do was to exclude the public from his life. The eventual result was that he achieved some degree of exclusivity, but at the expense of his marriage, his health and perhaps his sanity, and finally his life. Had there been someone else who might have been a model, Elvis might have had the humility, at least early in his life, to have learned from the experiences of others, but as it was, he led a life far from normal, seemingly even before he achieved stardom.

An early life during which he was spoiled and over-protected by his doting mother led into a brief period of just a few months of semi-normality as a truck driver, before rock'n'roll stardom beckoned, and Colonel Parker assumed the position only recently vacated by Gladys Presley, only sub-contracting the role of overlord and protector during Presley's army stint, until the formation of the Memphis Mafia, which saw Elvis surrounded largely by sycophants and yesmen. As a result of this, Elvis's grasp of what was normal was rarely, if ever, exercised. With a couple of exceptions, no one (after his mother's death) ever contradicted Elvis Presley. That one simple omission amounts to the greatest tragedy of all in rock'n'roll history.

BIBLIOGRAPHY

'Elvis: A Biography', Jerry Hopkins. US: Simon and Schusten.

'Elvis: The Final Years', Jerry Hopkins. US: St. Martin's Press; UK: W.H. Allen & Co.

'Elvis: The Complete Illustrated Record', Roy Carr and Mick Farren. US: Harmony Books; UK: Eel Pie Publishing.

'Elvis', Albert Goldman. US: McGraw Hill; UK: Allen Lane.

'Elvis', Dave Marsh. US: Rolling Stone Press; UK: Elm Tree Books.

'The Boy Who Dared To Rock: The Definitive Elvis', Paul Lichter. US: Doubleday Dolphin.

'When Elvis Died', Neal and Janice Gregory. US: Communications Press Inc.

'Elvis: The Films And Career Of Elvis Presley', Steven and Boris Zmijewsky. US: Citadel Press.

'Elvis In His Own Words', compiled by Mick Farren and Pearce Marchbank. US and UK: Omnibus Press.

'Elvis '56: In The Beginning', Alfred Wertheimer. US: Collier Books; UK: Cassell.

'Mystery Train', Greil Marcus. US: Dutton & Co Inc; UK: Omnibus Press.

'Elvis: What Happened?', Red West, Sonny West, Dave Hebler as told to Steve Dunleavy. US and UK: Ballantine.

'Elvis: We Love You Tender', Dee Presley, Billy, Rick and David Stanley. US: Delacorte, UK: New English Library.

'Up And Down With Elvis Presley', Marge Crumbaker with Gabe Tucker. US: G.P. Putnam's Sons; UK: New English Library.

'The Real Elvis: Good Old Boy', Vince Staten. US: Media Ventures Inc.

'Elvis: The Illustrated Discography', Martin Hawkins and Colin Escott. US and UK: Omnibus Press.

'All About Elvis', Fred L. Worth and Steve D. Tamerius. US: Bantam.

'The Complete Elvis', edited by Martin Torgoff. US: Delilah; UK: Virgin Books.

FILMOGRAPHY

'Love Me Tender'. Elvis plays Clint Reno; among the other stars are Debra Paget, Richard Egan and Neville Brand. Produced by David Weisbart and directed by Robert D. Webb for 20th Century-Fox; released in November 1956.

'Loving You'. Elvis plays Deke Rivers; other stars in the film include Lizabeth Scott, Wendell Corey and Dolores Hart. Produced by Hal B. Wallis and directed by Hal Kantner for Paramount; released in July 1957.

'Jailhouse Rock'. Elvis plays Vince Everett; his co-stars include Mickey Shaughnessy and Judy Tyler. Produced by Pandro S. Berman and directed by Richard Thorpe for M.G.M.; released during October 1957.

'King Creole'. Elvis plays Danny Fisher; the starstudded cast also features Carolyn Jones, Dolores Hart, Dean Jagger, Walter Matthau and Vic Morrow. Produced by Hal B. Willis and directed by Michael Curtiz for Paramount; released in June 1958.

'G.I. Blues'. Elvis plays Tulsa McLean; among the other stars are Juliet Prowse and James Douglas. Produced by Hal B. Wallis and directed by Norman Taurog for Paramount; released in October 1960.

'Flaming Star'. Elvis plays Pacer Burton; co-stars are Steve Forrest, Barbara Eden and Dolores Del Rio. Produced by David Weisbart and directed by Don Siegel for 20th Century-Fox; released in December 1960.

'Wild In The Country'. Elvis plays Glenn Tyler; the star-filled cast includes Hope Lange, Tuesday Weld, Rafer Johnson, John Ireland and Gary Lockwood. Produced by Jerry Wald and directed by Philip Dunne for 20th Century-Fox; released in June 1961.

'Blue Hawaii'. Elvis plays Chad Gates; supported by Joan Blackman and Angela Lansbury. Produced by Hal B. Wallis and directed by Norman Taurog for Paramount; released in November 1961.

'Follow That Dream'. Elvis plays Toby Kwimper; Arthur O'Connell and Anne Helm co-starred. Produced by David Weisbart and directed by Gordon Douglas for United Artists; released in March 1962.

'Kid Galahad'. Elvis plays Walter Gulick; with Gig Young, Lola Albright, Joan Blackman and Charles Bronson. Produced by David Weisbart and directed by Phil Karlson for United Artists; released in July 1962.

'Girls! Girls! Girls!'. Elvis plays Ross Carpenter; his co-stars include Stella Stevens, Laurel Goodwin and Jeremy Slate. Produced by Hal B. Wallis and directed by Norman Taurog, with associate producer Paul Nathan, for Paramount; released in November 1962.

'It Happened At The World's Fair'. Elvis plays Mike Edwards; also starring Joan O'Brien and Gary Lockwood. Produced by Ted Richmond and directed by Norman Taurog for M.G.M.; released in April 1963.

'Fun In Acapulco'. Elvis plays Mike Windgren; Ursula Andress co-stars. Produced by Hal B. Wallis and directed by Richard Thorpe for Paramount; released in November 1963.

'Kissin' Cousins'. Elvis plays both Josh Morgan and Jodie Tatum; supported by Arthur O'Connell and Glenda Farrell. Produced by Sam Katzman and directed by Gene Nelson for M.G.M.; released in March 1964.

'Viva Las Vegas'. Elvis plays Lucky Jordan; co-star Ann-Margret. Produced by Jack Cummings and George Sidney (who also directs) for M.G.M.; released in April 1964.

'Roustabout'. Elvis plays Charlie Rogers; co-starring Barbara Stanwyck, Joan Freeman and Leif Erickson. Produced by Hal B. Wallis with associated producer Paul Nathan and directed by John Rich for Paramount; released in November 1964.

'Girl Happy'. Elvis plays Rusty Wells; co-stars include Shelley Fabares, Harold J. Stone and Gary Crosby. Produced by Joe Pasternak and directed by Boris Segal for M.G.M.; released in January 1965.

'Tickle Me'. Elvis plays Lonnie Beale; co-stars Julie Adams, Jocelyn Lane and Jack Mullaney. Produced by Ben Schwalb and directed by Norman Taurog for Allied Artists; released in June 1965.

'Harum Scarum' (U.K. 'Harem Holiday'). Elvis plays Johnny Tyronne; with Mary Ann Mobley and Fran Jeffries. Produced by Sam Katzman and directed by Gene Nelson for M.G.M.; released in December 1965.

'Frankie And Johnny'. Elvis plays Johnny; Donna Douglas as Frankie and other stars include Nancy Kovack and Sue Ann Langdon. Produced by Edward Small and directed by Fred de Cordova for United Artists; released in July 1966.

'Paradise – Hawaiian Style'. Elvis plays Rick Richards; Suzanna Leigh and James Shigeta co-star. Produced by Hal B. Wallis, with associate producer Paul Nathan, and directed by Michael Moore for Paramount; released in June 1966.

'Spinout' (U.K. 'California Holiday'). Elvis plays Mike McCoy; supported by Shelley Fabares, Diane McBain and Deborah Walley. Produced by Joe Pasternak and directed by Norman Taurog for M.G.M.; released in December 1966.

'Easy Come, Easy Go'. Elvis plays Ted Jackson; other stars included Dodie Marshall and Elsa Lanchester. Produced by Hal B. Wallis with associate producer Paul Nathan and directed by John Rich for Paramount; released in June 1967.

'Double Trouble'. Elvis plays Guy Lambert; other stars include Annette Day, Yvonne Romain and Norman Rossington. Produced by Judd Bernard and Irwin Winkler and directed by Norman Taurog for M.G.M.; released in May 1967.

'Clambake'. Elvis plays Scott Heywood; co-stars include Shelley Fabares, Will Hutchins and Bill 'Incredible Hulk' Bixby. A Levy-Gardner-Laven production directed by Arthur Nadel for United Artists; released in December 1967.

'Stay Away, Joe'. Elvis plays Joe Lightcloud; with co-stars Burgess Meredith, Joan Blondell, Katy Jurado and Quentin Dean. Produced by Douglas Laurence and directed by Peter Tewkesbury for M.G.M.; released in March 1968.

'Speedway'. Elvis stars as Steve Grayson; with Nancy Sinatra and Bill Bixby again. Produced by Douglas Laurence and directed by Norman Taurog for M.G.M.; released in June 1968.

'Live A Little, Love A Little'. Elvis plays Greg; co-stars include Michele Carey, Rudy Vallee and pop star Eddie Hodges. Produced by Douglas Laurence and directed by veteran Presley movie man Norman Taurog for M.G.M.; released during October 1968.

'Charro'. Elvis plays Jesse Wade; co-stars Ina Balin and Victor French. Executive producer was Harry A. Caplan and the film was produced and directed by Charles M. Warren for National General Pictures; released in September 1969.

'The Trouble With Girls (And How To Get Into It)'. Elvis plays Walter Hale; among his co-stars are Marylyn Mason, Sheree North and John Anthony. Produced by Lester Welch and directed by Peter Tewkesbury for M.G.M.; released in December 1969.

'Change Of Habit'. Elvis plays Dr. John Carpenter; Mary Tyler Moore plays a nun, Sister Michelle, in this final fictional movie in which Elvis appeared. Produced by Joe Connelly and directed by William Graham for NBC-Universal; released during January 1970.

'Elvis – That's The Way It Is'. A documentary starring Elvis, relating to a performance at the International Hotel, Las Vegas. Produced by Dale Hutchinson and directed by Denis Sanders for M.G.M., and featuring Elvis performing 27 songs. Released in December 1970.

'Elvis On Tour'. Another documentary, but this time focusing on a tour. Produced and directed by Pierre Adidge and Robert Abel with associate producer Sidney Levin for M.G.M.; released in June 1973.

HIT SINGLE DISCOGRAPHY

Title	UK Chart Entry Date	Highest Position	US Chart Entry Date	Highest Position	Title	UK Chart Entry Date	Highest Position	US Chart Entry Date	Highest Position
Heartbreak Hotel	5/56	2	2/56	1	Wooden Heart	3/61	1		
I Was The One			3/56	19	Lonely Man			3/61	32
Blue Suede Shoes	5/56	9			Surrender	5/61	1	3/61	1
My Baby Left Me			6/56	31	Wild In The Country	9/61	4	6/61	26
I Want You, I Need You, I					I Feel So Bad			6/61	5
Love You	7/56	14	7/56	1	His Latest Flame	11/61	1	10/61	4
Hound Dog	9/56	2	8/56	1	Little Sister			11/61	5
Don't Be Cruel			9/56	1	Rock-A-Hula Baby	2/62	1	1/62	23
Blue Moon	11/56	9	10/56	55	Can't Help Falling In Love			1/62	2
Love Me Tender	12/56	11	11/56	1	Good Luck Charm	5/62	1	4/62	1
Anyway You Want Me			11/56	20	Anything That's Part Of				
Too Much	5/57	6	2/57	1	You			4/62	31
Playing For Keeps			2/57	21	She's Not You	8/62	1	9/62	5
Mystery Train	2/57	25			Just Tell Her Jim Said				
Rip It Up	3/57	27			Hello			9/62	55
All Shook Up	6/57	1	4/57	1	King Of The Whole Wide				
That's When Your					World			10/62	30
Heartaches Begin			4/57	58	Where Do You Come From			10/62	99
Teddy Bear	7/57	3	7/57	1	Return To Sender	11/62	1	11/62	2
Loving You	11/57	24	7/57	20	One Broken Heart For Sale	2/63	12	3/63	11
Paralysed	8/57	8			They Remind Me Too Much				
Party	10/57	2			Of You			3/63	53
Got A Lot O' Livin' To Do	10/57	17			Devil In Disguise	6/63	1	8/63	3
Trying To Get To You	11/57	16			Bossa Nova Baby	10/63	13	11/63	8
Lawdy Miss Clawdy	11/57	15			Kiss Me Quick	12/63	14	5/64	34
Jailhouse Rock	1/58	1	10/57	1	It Hurts Me			3/64	29
Treat Me Nice			10/57	18	Kissins' Cousins	6/64	10	3/64	12
Santa Bring My Baby Back					Viva Las Vegas	3/64	17	6/64	29
To Me	11/57	7			What'd I Say			6/64	21
I'm Left, You're Right,					Such A Night	8/64	13	8/64	16
She's Gone	1/58	21			Ain't That Lovin' You				
Don't	2/58	2	2/58	1	Baby	10/64	15	11/64	16
I Beg Of You			2/58	8	Ask Me			11/64	12
Wear My Ring Around					Blue Christmas	12/64	11		
Your Neck	5/58	3	5/58	2	Do The Clam	3/65	19	4/65	21
Doncha' Think It's Time			5/58	15	Crying In The Chapel	5/65	1	6/65	3
Hard Headed Woman	7/58	2	7/58	1	(Such An) Easy Question			7/65	11
Don't Ask Me Why			7/58	25	It Feels So Right			7/65	55
King Creole	10/58	2			I'm Yours			10/65	11
One Night	1/59	1	12/58	4	Tell Me Why	11/65	15	1/66	33
I Got Stung			12/58	8	Puppet On A String			12/65	14
A Fool Such As I	4/59	1	5/59	2	Blue River	2/66	22	1/66	95
I Need Your Love Tonight			5/59	4	Frankie And Johnny	4/66	21	4/66	25
A Big Hunk O' Love	7/59	4	8/59	1	Please Don't Stop Loving				
My Wish Came True			8/59	12	Me			4/66	45
Stuck On You	4/60	3	5/60	1	Love Letters	7/66	6	7/66	19
Fame And Fortune			5/60	17	All That I Am	10/66	18	11/66	41
A Mess Of Blues	7/60	2	9/60	32	Spinout			11/66	40
It's Now Or Never	11/60	1	9/60	1	If Every Day Was Like				
Are You Lonesome Tonight	1/61	1	12/60	1	Christmas	12/66	13		
I Gotta Know			12/60	20	Indescribably Blue	2/67	21	2/67	33

184

Title	UK Chart Entry Date	Highest Position	US Chart Entry Date	Highest Position
That's Someone You Never Forget			5/67	92
You Gotta Stop/Love Machine	5/67	38		
Long Legged Girl (With The Short Dress On)			6/67	63
There's Always Me			9/67	56
Judy			9/67	78
Big Boss Man			11/67	38
You Don't Know Me			11/67	44
Guitar Man	2/68	19	2/68	43
Stay Away			4/68	67
You'll Never Walk Alone	10/68	44	4/68	90
U.S. Male	5/68	15	5/68	28
Your Time Hasn't Come Yet Baby	7/68	22	7/68	72
Let Yourself Go			7/68	71
A Little Less Conversation			10/68	69
Almost In Love			10/68	95
If I Can Dream	2/69	11	1/69	12
Memories			4/69	35
In The Ghetto	6/69	2	6/69	3
Clean Up Your Own Backyard	9/69	21	8/69	35
Suspicious Minds	10/69	1	11/69	2
Don't Cry Daddy	2/70	8	1/70	6
Rubberneckin'			1/70	69
Kentucky Rain	5/70	21	5/70	16
The Wonder Of You	7/70	1	6/70	9
Mama Liked The Roses			6/70	65
I've Lost You	11/70	9	8/70	32
The Next Step Is Love			8/70	33
You Don't Have To Say You Love Me	1/71	9	11/70	11
Patch It Up			11/70	90
I Really Don't Want To Know			1/71	21
There Goes My Everything	3/71	6	1/71	57
Rags To Riches	5/71	9	4/71	45
Where Did They Go Lord			4/71	33
Life			6/71	53
Only Believe			6/71	95
Heartbreak Hotel/Hound Dog (reissue)	7/71	10		
I'm Leavin'	10/71	23	8/71	36
It's Only Love			10/71	51
I Just Can't Help Believing	12/71	6		
Until It's Time For You To Go	4/72	5	3/72	40
American Trilogy	6/72	8	5/72	66
Burning Love	9/72	7	10/72	2
Always On My Mind	12/72	9		
Separate Ways			1/73	20
Steamroller Blues			5/73	17
Fool	8/73	15	5/73	79
Polk Salad Annie	5/73	23		
Raised On Rock	11/73	26	10/73	41
For Ol' Times Sake			10/73	95
I've Got A Thing About You Baby	3/74	33	3/74	39
Take Good Care Of Her			3/74	63
If You Talk In Your Sleep	7/74	40	8/74	17
My Boy	11/74	5	3/75	20
Promised Land	1/75	9	12/74	14
T.R.O.U.B.L.E.	5/75	31	6/75	35
Green Green Grass Of Home	11/75	29		
Bringing It Back	11/75	65		
For The Heart			4/76	95
Hurt	5/76	37	5/76	28
Girl Of My Best Friend	9/76	9		
Suspicion	12/76	9		
Moody Blue	3/77	6	2/77	31
She Thinks I Still Care			2/77	95
Way Down	8/77	1	9/77	18
It's Now Or Never (reissue)	9/77	39		
All Shook Up (reissue)	9/77	41		
Crying In The Chapel (reissue)	9/77	43		
Jailhouse Rock (reissue)	9/77	44		
Are You Lonesome Tonight (reissue)	9/77	46		
The Wonder Of You (reissue)	9/77	48		
Wooden Heart (reissue)	9/77	49		
Return To Sender (reissue)	9/77	42		
My Way	12/77	9	12/77	22
Don't Be Cruel (reissue)	6/78	24		
It Won't Seem Like Christmas (Without You)	12/79	13		
It's Only Love/Beyond The Reef	8/80	3		
Santa Claus Is Back In Town	12/80	41		
Guitar Man (new version)	2/81	43	1/81	39
Loving Arms	4/81	47		
Are You Lonesome Tonight (laughing version)	3/82	25		
Jailhouse Rock (reissue)	2/83	27		

NB: The American charts are compiled from both radio play and sales, and on several occasions both sides of Elvis's singles made the listings. This didn't happen in the U.K. where sales are compiled from record sales only, and it is usual for the record company's chosen 'A' side to be listed.

ESSENTIAL ALBUM DISCOGRAPHY

Compiling an 'essential discography' has been difficult because Elvis's RCA catalogue is muddled and untidy, and while there are several good collections of 'Greatest Hits', there is no box-set or LP series that satisfactorily gathers together the best from his twenty-three-year recording career. The disorganization of Presley's records can be traced back to the mid-1950s when it was discovered that fans would buy almost anything with Elvis's name on it, so numerous repackaging projects were carried out with the finest material spread thinly over several LPs, and it's still impossible to buy every good Elvis recording without ending up with several copies of some of the best-known songs, plus a lot of unwelcome dross. There are other problems, such as different track listings on albums with the same title – for example: *A Date With Elvis* has been issued twice in Britain with the same cover but a different song selection – or, conversely, LPs with totally different names and covers in the U.S. and U.K. but identical contents. We therefore recommend that you check the contents of records before purchase, perhaps after consulting one of the reliable discographies (Carr & Farren, Hawkins & Escott). Serious efforts to re-release Elvis's best work in a methodical and intelligent manner have been confined to the early years, with *The Elvis Presley Sun Collection* and *The '56 Sessions*, both of which originated in the U.K., and it's worth noting that they didn't appear until twenty years after the recordings were made, so we shall probably have to wait a long while for a *Best Of Elvis* collection that finally does justice to the man and his music. The recommended albums are listed in order of release, with the date of origin but the most recent RCA catalogue number.

America	Great Britain
Elvis Presley 1956 AFL 1–1254	*Rock'n'Roll. No. 1* 1956 INTS 5148. Elvis's first LP was issued in the U.K. on the H.M.V. label with the same cover as the American debut but with a new title and some different tracks. The LP was re-issued in 1972 in re-channelled stereo. These tracks sound best in the original mono on *The '56 Sessions* and *The Elvis Presley Sun Collection* albums listed below.
Elvis 1956 AFL 1–1382	*Rock'n'Roll. No. 2* 1957 INTS 5142. Elvis's second LP is identical to the American version except for the title.
Loving You 1957 AFL 1–1515	*Loving You* 1977 INTS 5109. Eight of the tracks from the American album were issued in the U.K. on a 10-inch LP, the first Elvis album release on the British RCA label, but it was twenty years before the record was released in Britain in its original form.
Elvis' Christmas Album 1957 CAS 2428	*Elvis' Christmas Album* 1957 INTS 5060
Elvis' Golden Records Volume 1 1958 AFL 1–1707	*Elvis' Golden Records Volume 1* 1958 INTS 5143
King Creole 1958 AFL 1–1884	*King Creole* 1958 INTS 5103
For LP Fans Only 1958 AFL 1–1990	The records *For LP Fans Only* and *A Date With Elvis* contained previously released tracks that hadn't appeared on an album. *For LP Fans Only* was issued in the U.K. as *Elvis* with some track alterations, while *A Date With Elvis* appeared with the same title but with some different tracks. They are no longer 'essential' in Britain because the best material can be found on *The '56 Sessions* and *The Elvis Presley Sun Collection* compilations, listed below, which have only been issued in the U.K.
A Date With Elvis 1959 AFL 1–2011	

America	Great Britain
50,000,000 Elvis Fans Can't Be Wrong/Elvis' Gold Records Volume 2 1959 AFL 1–2075	*Elvis' Golden Records Volume 2* 1959 INTS 5144
Elvis Is Back 1960 AFL 1–2231	*Elvis Is Back* 1960 INTS 5141
His Hand In Mine 1960 AFL 1–1319	*His Hand In Mine* 1960 INTS 5105
Elvis' Golden Records Volume 3 1963 AFL 1–2765	*Elvis' Golden Records Volume 3* 1963 INTS 5145
How Great Thou Art 1967 AFL 1–3758	*How Great Thou Art* 1967 INTS 5147
Elvis' Golden Records Volume 4 1968 AFL 1–3921	*Elvis' Golden Records Volume 4* 1968 INTS 5146
Elvis – TV Special 1968 AFM 1–4088	*Elvis – TV Special* 1968 INTS 5093
From Elvis In Memphis 1969 AFL 1–4155	*From Elvis In Memphis* 1969 SF 8029
From Memphis To Vegas/From Vegas To Memphis 1969 LSP 6020	*From Memphis To Vegas/From Vegas To Memphis* 1969 SF 8080/81
Worldwide 50 Gold Award Hits Volume 1 1970 LPM 6401 This is a 4-LP box set containing Elvis's biggest hits from the Fifties and Sixties.	*Worldwide 50 Gold Award Hits Volume 1* 1970 LPM 6401
Elvis Country (I'm 10,000 Years Old) 1971 AFL 1–4460	*Elvis Country (I'm 10,000 Years Old)* 1971 INTS 5111
Elvis – A Legendary Performer. Volume 1 1974 CPL 1–0341 A collection of greatest hits and some previously unreleased material.	*Elvis – A Legendary Performer. Volume 1* 1974 CPL 1–0341
	Elvis' 40 Greatest 1974 PL42691(2). A joint release between RCA and Arcade, this double album set featured Elvis's biggest hits. RCA in Britain have subsequently issued the collection on two separate LPs, listed below.
	Hits Of The Seventies 1974 LPL 1–7527. A collection of Elvis's best recordings from the early Seventies.
Elvis Today 1975 AFL 1–1039	*Elvis Today* 1975 RS 1011
The Sun Sessions 1976 APM 1–1675 An identical selection of Elvis's Sun recordings, but with a different title and cover, was released first in the U.K. then in the U.S.A.	*The Elvis Presley Sun Collection* 1975 NL 42757
Elvis – A Legendary Performer. Volume 2 1976 CPL 1–1349	*Elvis – A Legendary Performer. Volume 2* 1976 CPL 1–1349

America	Great Britain

America

Moody Blue 1977 AFL 1–2428
A weak album only listed because it features the songs *Moody Blue* and *Way Down*.

Elvis – A Legendary Performer. Volume 3 1979 CPL 1–3082

Elvis Aron Presley 1980 CPL 83699 An eight-album box set, which provided good historical value but less good value for money.

This Is Elvis 1981 CPL 2–4031 An LP tied in with the 'This Is Elvis' movie, it included previously unreleased material from T.V. shows, plus hits like *Promised Land* and *Moody Blue* which hadn't been reissued too often.

Great Britain

Moody Blue 1977 RCALP 3021

Elvis – The '56 Sessions Volume 1 1978 RCALP 3025. Every song Elvis recorded in 1956 is featured on this album and its companion listed below.

Elvis – A Legendary Performer. Volume 3 1979 PL 13082

Elvis – The '56 Sessions Volume 2 1979 RCALP 3030

Elvis Presley Sings Leiber & Stoller 1980 INTS 5031

This Is Elvis 1981 LP 5029

20 Greatest Hits. Volume 1 1981 INTS 5115

20 Greatest Hits. Volume 2 1981 INTS 5116. These two budget-price reissues contain the same songs as *Elvis' 40 Greatest*.

INDEX